DEFENDING YOUR BRAND
AGAINST IMITATION

Defending Your Brand against Imitation

Consumer Behavior, Marketing Strategies, and Legal Issues

Judith Lynne Zaichkowsky

Q

QUORUM BOOKS
Westport, Connecticut • London

Library of Congress Cataloging-in-Publication Data

Zaichkowsky, Judith Lynne, 1951–
    Defending your brand against imitation : consumer behavior,
marketing strategies, and legal issues / Judith Lynne Zaichkowsky.
      p.   cm.
    Includes bibliographical references and index.
    ISBN 0–89930–829–5 (alk. paper)
    1. Brand name products—Marketing—Management.
2. Consumer behavior. 3. Trademarks. 4. Industrial property.
5. Marketing—Law and legislation. 6. Imitation—Case studies.
I. Title.
HF5415.13.Z35 1995
658.8'27—dc20   94–31462

British Library Cataloguing in Publication Data is available.

Library of Congress Catalog Card Number: 94–31462
ISBN: 0–89930–829–5

First published in 1995

Quorum Books, 88 Post Road West, Westport, CT 06881
An imprint of Greenwood Publishing Group, Inc.

Printed in the United States of America

The paper used in this book complies with the
Permanent Paper Standard issued by the National
Information Standards Organization (Z39.48–1984).

10 9 8 7 6 5 4 3 2 1

To the memory of one great father
John Zaichkowsky 1920–1984

Contents

Illustrations

TABLES

FIGURES

EXHIBITS

Preface

The main intent of this book is to provide a broad background to the concept of brand imitation. Brands are defined, in the broadest sense of the word, as people, as well as objects or ideas, that are subject to the act of others imitating them. Preventing and stopping competitors and others from imitating is a difficult task. While this book may not provide all the answers, it will certainly inform the reader of the complexities of the issues of brand imitation.

It is quite likely that you have been prompted to buy this book after finding the unpleasant situation that someone has infringed on your trademark. The first thing you should do, of course, is obtain experienced legal counsel. You may already have excellent legal counsel and they have turned you to this book for some background information to brand imitation.

The important factor is to take some action against unethical competitors who copy another business's identity. Do not ignore them. To ignore brand imitation is to condone it. Condoning it is likely to breed future brand imitation. The ideal strategy is to prevent brand imitation in the first place. The possibility of brand imitation should be contemplated when designing new products or brand packaging. To try to stop brand imitation once it appears in the marketplace is difficult and costly. It is the intent of this book to provide those involved in commerce with some understanding, some ideas, and perhaps some strategy on building differentiated and protectable brands.

It is difficult to be specific about the usefulness of this book to the audience, because there are many different audiences for this broad subject. Brand managers, intellectual property attorneys, market researchers, consumers, and academics all have very different needs and interests, yet there is an area of interest in this book for each segment. The different chapters may be of use to different groups. For example, lawyers may find Chapters 2 and 3 on consumer behavior the most useful and interesting. Market researchers may find Chapter 6, on testing for brand imitation, a good source of ideas. Brand managers may find Chapter 5 on being distinctive, beneficial for designing packaging and marketing strategy. Academics may find Chapter 4, which attempts to categorize trademark infringement cases by cues, a good source of ideas for future research.

In attempting to convey the whole picture of brand imitation, this book takes a risk in not targeting one audience. I do not know how smart a marketer I've been with my own book in trying to appeal to all involved in brand imitation. I may have not really pleased any one segment. Yet to quote Bill Wells via Dennis Rook, "Progress comes in the gaps between disciplines." I have certainly attempted to expose those gaps.

Acknowledgments

Getting a book to the publisher is a major feat. This process lasted over three years and could have easily lasted another three years without threats of final(!) deadlines. I easily missed three dates for getting the manuscript to the publisher. Therefore the first person I would like to thank is Eric Valentine for his patience with me. Writing a monograph while teaching full time and organizing a department is very difficult. Time only comes in short periods, and constantly picking up pieces of work here and there does not lead to fluid thought on the issues. I also admit to spending a great deal of time traveling and presenting papers in Australia, Europe, and North America during the three years. This has definitely helped delay the finishing of the monograph, but at the same time I learned that brand imitation is a global marketing problem, and companies all over the world have to deal with protecting their brand identity and image.

But as Charles Hofacker, a colleague, once relayed to me, "A manuscript is never finished; someone just comes and takes it away from you." So the final deadline has come and you are left to read what is started. The reader will realize the importance of this statement when he or she finishes reading the monograph and comes to think about all the questions arising from the work. There is much to be learned and researched with respect to brand imitation.

The people who brought me into this area are lawyers Rees Brock, Q. C., and Michelle McPhee. It was a fascinating experience to be brought into the world of law and the courtroom. Their patience with me, their support, and their trust in me was the pinnacle of professional interaction. I believe we learned a great deal of each other's world, and the experience left me with the highest regard for the legal profession. It also left me with the knowledge that there was a great need for some source book in the area of passing-off that a non-lawyer involved in the issue could read and understand.

The one person who has influenced me most in this direction is my mentor, Hal Kassarjian. Before retiring, he taught marketing and the law for years at UCLA. He has acted as a consultant and expert witness for the smallest to the largest corporations and governments. It was his files, his office, his computer, and his comments that have been the source and basis for much of this book. His generosity of time and ideas are always an inspiration to me.

Rob Donovan of the University of Western Australia, who also runs a marketing research firm and routinely does research into brand imitation, gave invaluable contributions and criticisms. Dennis Rook of the University of Southern California read the full first draft and gave me ideas and encouragement on strengthening the monograph. Jean-Noël Kapferer of H.E.C. Paris, who also does research in the area of brand confusion, provided more support and ideas for research. I thank Stan Shapiro, dean of business at Simon Fraser University, for not only his comments on strengthening the manuscript but also for his tolerance of my absences to Los Angeles, where I arranged blocks of time to write the monograph.

There are too many companies to name that I have talked to over the past three years, with regard to brand imitation. However, my meeting with Lego was most beneficial. Lego has a team of sixteen lawyers on site who deal with thirty to forty cases of trademark infringement in ten to fifteen countries at any one time. Sten Juul Petersen provided me with documents and information that were very useful to this book.

I would also like to thank my graduate students Neil Simpson and Roberta Hupman for working with me in this area. None of their studies are reported in this book, but their work on experience with imitators and ethical perspectives represents a start to an academic understanding of consumers and how they relate to brand imitation. My right-hand research assistant, Susan Dyson, was invaluable to me throughout the preparation of the monograph. She carefully read every word twice, edited, and provided questions to clarify my writing. Betty Chung and Graham Hunter prepared the tables, figures, and exhibits while I constantly changed them. Thank you all for your time, patience, knowledge, and support.

DEFENDING YOUR BRAND AGAINST IMITATION

1

Understanding and Protecting Brand Identity

Intentionally integrating the name, the shape, the symbol, the color, and/or the look associated with a successful brand to a new brand on the marketplace may shift sales away from the original brand to the new brand. This shift occurs because consumers may be led by similar cues to believe that the two brands are interchangeable. Although it is difficult to assess the dollar value of the infringement, an industry source states, "a private label item that knocks off a branded item selling 1000 cases a week can expect to do 400–500 cases a week within six months" (Fitzell 1982: 111). In an economic study of forty-five companies with worldwide sales of $113.2 billion, lost profits to foreign infringers were estimated to be $2.1 billion (Feinberg and Rousslang 1990). In addition to the possible monetary loss to original manufacturers, there is a potential reduction in the perception of quality or image of the original due to infringing brands that are cheaper and/or of inferior quality.

Therefore, the producers of successful established brands should be motivated to protect the distinctive identity of their products and their brand equity by prosecuting possible infringers under trademark laws. However, a survey among European companies manufacturing branded products showed that more than 80 percent of the respondents had seen some of their products imitated at least once within the preceding five years. Only about half of them had taken legal steps against the imitators, citing cumbersome procedures, high costs, and uncertainty of outcomes because of widely varying practices as the main reasons for not defending their brand against imitators (Lego Group 1994).

Counterfeiting is relatively easy to identify. A counterfeit is a 100 percent direct copy. However, imitation is not necessarily a direct copy and is therefore more difficult to define, identify, label as illegal, and hence prevent. Brand imitation deals with similarities, not differences. What is similar is sometimes more a matter of individual perception than of reality. What may be perceived and defined as an illegal offering in the marketplace by some may not be perceived and defined as such by others.

Determining what exactly makes a brand similar and desirable to copy is not always obvious and varies greatly among brands and product. Since litigation is costly, managers should be aware of the various types of cues consumers use to identify brands and how these cues transfer association and meaning, not only to competing brands but to related products or even unrelated product categories.

This book focuses on similarity of trademarks and trade dress with the intent of providing background information on consumer choice behavior; psychological forces behind the issue of imitation; and a review of selected court cases in which different cues were the basis for brand identification. It is the similarity of trademarks that is germane to cueing consumer expectations. The understanding of what causes perceived similarity, how to label it, how to avoid it, and how to test for its existence is important in the decision of taking a possible infringer to court and perhaps preventing any future infringing competitors.

BACKGROUND TO THE PROBLEM

The distinctive identity of products and services has enormous commercial importance. It protects the goodwill of the name of the firm, identifies the source of the manufactured goods, and helps consumers draw conclusions about the goods purchased. These distinctive features include cues of brand name, style of lettering, background, shape, symbols, color, and Gestalt or the general look that is learned by the consuming public over time through the process of purchase and use, from conversations, and from advertisements. Consumers use these distinctive features or cues to short-cut cognitive processing of the goods they buy to make their shopping more efficient. The courts have recognized this fact for many years, as evidenced in the following statement from Mr. Justice Frankfurter in *Mishawaka Rubber and Woolen Mfg. Co. v. S. S. Kresge Co.* (1942):

The protection of trade marks is the law's recognition of the psychological function of symbols. If it is true that we live by symbols, it is no less true that we purchase goods by them. A trademark is a merchandising short-cut which induces a purchaser to select what he wants, or what he has been led to believe he wants. The owner of a mark exploits this human propensity by making every effort to impregnate the atmosphere of the market with the drawing power of a congenial symbol. Whatever the means employed, the aim is the same—to convey through the mark, in the minds of the potential customers, the desirability of the commodity upon which it appears. Once this is attained, the trade mark owner has something of value. If another poaches upon the commercial magnetism of the symbol he has created, the owner can obtain legal redress. The creation of a mark through an established symbol implies that people float on a psychological current engendered by the various advertising devices which give a trade mark its potency. (Bowen 1961: 6–7)

The establishment of the trademark, as a merchandising short-cut, is more than just registration. Trademarks acquire a degree of fame through their extensive and widespread use over time. Therefore, brand identification by trademark or trade dress is not only important for choice, but is also very important for the meaning associated with the identifying cue. Trademarks are dynamic pieces of property that become stronger with extensive widespread continuous use, but wilt with interrupted small-scale use.

TRADEMARKS

What are they?

Trademarks are types of intellectual property consisting of a term, symbol, design, or combination of these cues to give protection to the identification of a business or a product. Trademarks may be derived from various sources. The mark may come from a coined word, such as Exxon or Kodak. It may be an ordinary word that has no apparent meaning in connection with the product to which it is attached, such as Arrow dress shirts. It may be a descriptive word that suggests the performance of the product, such as Mr Clean. It could be a foreign name, like Lux; a founder's name, Ford; the name of a historically famous person, Lincoln; numerals, No. 5 perfume; a picture, such as Elsie the Cow for Bordens; or a shape, such as the Coca-Cola bottle (Levy and Rook 1981). Trademarks can be as diverse as the imagination of the manufacturer. The mechanisms underlying the development of trademarks are articulated by Cohen (1986, 1991) under trademark planning and product decisions.

Legal Aspects

The guidelines for registration of trademarks and the specific laws that protect trademarks can be found in legal doctrines of the country. Some of these laws are briefly outlined in the Appendix. Because the specific laws vary from country to country, change from time to time, and all laws are open to interpretation and judgment, it is difficult to specify what is legal and illegal. Counterfeiting is definitely illegal, but brand imitation is not necessarily counterfeiting as it does not actually imply a direct copy. This book is not written from a legal perspective but provides a guide on how to understand the concept of brand imitation from the perspective of the physical cues and how the consumer perceives these physical cues for identification and association.

Applying for trademark registration is a complicated process, and anyone doing so should acquire the services of a lawyer specializing in trademarks. Readers interested in the legal aspects of trademarks should consult the written law in their own country: the Federal Trademarks Act in the United States; the Trademarks Act (1985) in Canada; and the International Trademark Agreement governing the sale of goods internationally. However, the concept of an "international brand" is not yet a legal reality, because there is no one mechanism for registering a trademark all around the globe (Kapferer 1992).

The general purpose of trademark legislation is to prevent others from using distinctive marks that will confuse people into thinking they are dealing with the owner of the trademark when they are not. When a party makes use of a trademark belonging to another, it is up to the original owners of the mark to convince the court of two points: first, that they actually own the trademark, and second, that it is likely that the public has been or will be confused by the wrongful use of the trademark. It is the intent of this book to provide information with respect to the second point.

Passing-off

The term passing-off is used to describe the situation in which people confuse one business or one product with another. The common law of passing-off prevents a person from misleading consumers into thinking that they are dealing with some other business or person when they are not. The person being harmed can ask the court to order compensation or to stop the offending conduct. To succeed in a passing-off action, it is necessary to establish that the public was misled (Yates 1989).

However, it is not necessary to show that the defendant *intended* to mislead or confuse the public. For example, a case involving cat litter (*A & M Pet Products Inc. v. Pieces Inc.* and *Royal K-9*, 1989) found that customers purchased the imitator brand thinking that it was the original. The imitator brand had a similarly shaped container, and customers testified that they just assumed it was the same product from the same manufacturer when in fact it was not. There was no actual evidence that the manufacturer intended to mislead the consumer.

WHAT IS CONFUSION?

Consumer Confusion

In the eyes of the law, "consumer confusion results when two marks stimulate substantially identical psychological reactions in the minds of the purchasers when they see the marks on the goods, and a mental association is created as between the involved products or their producers" (Leeds 1956: 5). This means that the consumer can be well aware that the two objects in question are not identical. The consumer only has to draw similar inferences from each based on the distinctive features that are common to both items. This is exemplified in *Vidal Sassoon Inc. v. Beverly Sassoon and Slim Lines Inc.* (1982), where a consumer survey found that most purchasers of the Slim Lines Contour Gel thought it was manufactured by Vidal Sassoon, who is widely known for his hair care products. It was not, but most consumers interviewed deduced that it was due to the name of Beverly Sassoon printed on the jar. Most consumers focused solely on the familiar name of Sassoon and conjured up images of the hair care company.

Consumer Mistake

It is also possible that the consumer could make a mistake between the two objects in question because of their similarity. A consumer mistake results "when two marks sound so much alike or look so much alike that one product is purchased when the other is intended" (Leeds 1956: 5). In this case the consumer is not aware, at least at first, that a wrong purchase is made. These cases are usually confined to competing brands within a product category. For example in *Levi Strauss v. Blue Bell Inc.* (1980), a survey of purchasers of casual clothing showed that many consumers used a small tab to identify clothing as being manufactured by Levi. Because the competition was also using this small tab, it was deemed likely that consumers might mistakenly purchase the competitor's product and only later realize it was not Levi's. Lego, a Danish company that manufactures children's building blocks and other toys, constantly receives letters of complaint about their building blocks from customers who have bought imitators' building blocks. The consumers think that they are complaining about the Lego building blocks, a clear indication of a consumer mistake.

Consumer Deception

While confusion and mistake are rooted in the consumer, deception is rooted in the seller of the imitator goods. According to Leeds (1956: 5), consumer deception results when two marks engender the same psychological impression, or look so much alike, or sound so much alike that unscrupulous dealers are led to believe that they can sell the second user's good for those of the first without fear of detection, or if detected, with an excuse believed sufficient to excuse the action.

A case that might exemplify deception is *Hartford House Ltd. v. Hallmark Cards Inc.* (1986). In this case, even the manufacturer of the original brand was deceived by the imitator. Court documents showed that Hallmark deliberately set out to eliminate Hartford House as a competitor with its imitator product.

A consumer can be confused, make a mistake, or suffer from a deceptive practice with respect to products or services involving manufacturers; the source of the goods; or sponsorship or association (Boal 1983). While confusion and mistake are discovered from the point of view of the consumer, deception is rooted in the intent of the seller of the good. It is the seller or manufacturer of brand imitators who causes consumer confusion by the use of similar cues in the selling of their products. Marketers who do not want to confuse brands but want to sell in the same product category go to great lengths to provide the consumer with cues that are distinctive from their competitors.

The factors that the court considers in ruling on consumer confusion vary from court to court and from case to case. Anthony Fletcher (1989), in reviewing the different courts in the United States, came to the conclusion that there was very little agreement among the circuits on what factors to consider for the determination of confusion. Given that the courts may deal with confusion, mistake, and deception differently, it is not too surprising there is such disagreement. A summary of the main factors used for consideration of confusion are outlined in the Appendix under the various trademark acts.

Secondary Meaning

Secondary meaning is a legal term that is used from time to time in discussing brand confusion. It is the notion that a trademark or trade dress need not identify the source of a product by name, but rather that the look of the product provides the consumer with similar expectations. There appears to be three levels of secondary meaning (Palladino 1983: 1) liberal, in which the trademark or dress identifies one product; 2) accepted, in which the trademark or dress identifies the product of one, perhaps anonymous company; and 3) conservative, in which the trademark or dress identifies one specific company.

Secondary meaning, in the liberal sense, has been applied to drugs. For example, a company that produces a drug and packages it in a certain color has no ownership of the particular color of the particular drug. All drugs may be of that color, despite the origin or manufacturer (see *Inwood Laboratories Inc. v. Ives Laboratories Inc.,* 1982). An example of color in the conservative interpretation is *Eastman Kodak Co. v. Fotomat Corp.* (1971). Here Fotomat was enjoined from using the same colors on its buildings that Kodak used on its film. The court ruled that the color combination could only mean Kodak to the customer. In all cases the trademark or trade dress is identified with a source and, because of the source, the consumer has reason to buy rather than because of any concrete feature or attribute of the product.

The determination of secondary meaning may be through long and extensive use of a product or service; size or prominence of a business; success of promotional efforts by manufacturers; or by direct evidence such as consumer research (Fletcher 1989). For an extensive legal discussion and review of trademarks and secondary meaning, the reader is referred to an article on the subject by J. S. Armstrong (1992).

BRAND IMITATION AND BRAND EQUITY

A brand image has both a direct effect on sales and a moderating effect on the relationship between strategies and sales. . . . A brand image is not simply a perceptual phenomenon affected by the firm's communication activities alone. It is the understanding consumers derive from the total set of brand-related activities engaged in by the firm. (Park, Jaworski, and MacInnis 1986: 135)

The understanding of brand image explains the strong relationship between brand and perceived quality. The brand-perceived quality link explains the strategy of brand equity, or the extensions of present product lines and brands to other related products, unrelated products, or just association to the brand name itself.

Almost half of all packaged goods are brand extensions. This is due to the great amount of financial risk involved in entering new markets. Launching a new brand can cost upward of $80 million (Tauber 1988). A firm that imitates a competing brand's look is using the competitor's brand identity for its own benefit. For the imitating brand, this imitation strategy reduces the costs involved in launching a brand and creating a demand for it (Ward et al. 1986).

If the imitation brands are of lower quality, as they usually are (Fenby 1983; Carratu 1987), purchasers may devalue the original brand if they are not aware that the good is not the original or made by the original manufacturer. Lego finds itself in this position with respect to customers who are not aware that they have purchased an imitation of Lego building blocks. Lego's long-term concern here is that consumers will devalue the whole product category of building blocks and quit purchasing those kind of toys.

On the other hand, if the consumer is aware of the purchase of the imitation and is satisfied with the brand, then the consumer may devalue the original brand (Simpson 1992). This devaluation occurs because a cheaper yet adequate substitute has been found. Therefore, brand imitation may have very harmful effects to the equity of the original brand as it devalues the unique image, and hence the quality perception of the original brand name.

These problems may also occur when the brand name is taken to related or unrelated product categories by manufacturers other than the original. Products of poor quality or poor taste may be associated with the original brand. Therefore, brand imitation may have very harmful effects on the equity of the brand. From a marketing strategy point of view, certain brand extensions may be a necessary, although not necessarily desirable defense. Brand extensions may be used to block the use of the brand name by a third party in another product category. For example, Cartier, the elegant French jeweler, extended its name to textiles and tableware. This was a defensive strategy to prevent an Italian firm from registering the Cartier brand in these categories at an international level (Kapferer 1992). Christian Dior, a French fashion house, registered its name in the product category of cigarettes in 1955 (Fletcher 1989). Whether that was truly a defensive strategy at the time is hard to assess, but it does exemplify the protective strategy of taking one's brand name to unrelated product categories.

Diluting brand equity through unauthorized association and sponsorship is another major problem, not only of brands but also of organizations and individuals. The concern here may be the unwelcome association as well as the threat of confusion. Undermining the positive image or equity can lead to diminishing distinctiveness, uniqueness, effectiveness, or prestigious connotations. For example, the court held that the use of the name Tiffany's by a Boston night club harmed the New York jeweler's mark (*Tiffany & Co. v. Boston Club Inc.*, 1964). The National Hockey League found itself in court objecting to its unauthorized portrayal in advertising by PepsiCola (*National Hockey League v. PepsiCola Canada Ltd.*, 1992). Protecting one's image is important business because images take years to build, but can be destroyed rather quickly.

SUMMARY

Too often marketing competitors choose to imitate a very successful brand through their trademark or trade dress in order to appropriate some goodwill that already exists in the marketplace. This practice may harm the original seller in several ways. First, when the confusion involves competing brands, there may be some economic loss to the original producer or supplier as some consumers divert their purchases. These diversions can be conscious, in that the consumers know they are not purchasing the original. Second, some diversions are a real mistake on the part of the consumer at the point of purchase. If consumers never become aware of the mistake and the good is inferior, they may never purchase the good again because they believe the quality to be unacceptable.

Third, manufacturers or suppliers should also be alarmed when a seller of an unrelated good relies on their well-known trademark or trade dress in selling a good in a different product category. Although they are selling non-competing products, the brand equity of the original brand may be expropriated or even eroded by selling in another product or service category. This also applies to unrelated goods in the form of unauthorized sponsorship or association.

The basis for laws protecting trademarks or trade dress is the realization that they are valuable properties of the owners. Trademarks are the identifying cues for customers for choice and evaluation. They provide assurances of quality, warranty, satisfaction, and authenticity to the consumer.

REFERENCES

A & M Pet Products Inc. v. Pieces Inc. and *Royal K-9*, South West United States District Court, Central District of Los Angeles, case No. 89–4923 (1989).

Armstrong, J. S. (1992). Secondary meaning "in the making" in trademark infringement actions under Section 43(a) of the Lanham Act. *George Mason University Law Review*, 14 (Summer), No. 3, 603–35.

Boal, R. B. (1973). Techniques for ascertaining likelihood of confusion and the meaning of advertising communications. *Trademark Reporter*, *Vol. 73*, 405–35.

Bowen, D. C. (1961). Applied psychology and trademarks. *Trademark Reporter*, *Vol. 51*, 1–26.

Carratu, V. (1987). Commercial counterfeiting. In J. M. Murphy (ed.), *Branding: A Key Marketing Tool*. London: Macmillian Press, pp. 59–72.

Cohen, D. (1986). Trademark strategy. *Journal of Marketing*, 50 (January), 61–74.

———. (1991). Trademark strategy revisited. *Journal of Marketing*, 55 (July), 46–59.

Eastman Kodak Co. v. Fotomat Corp., 317 F. Supp. 304 N.D. Ga. 1969, appeal 441 F. 2d 1079 5th Cir. (1971).

Feinberg, R. M. and Rousslang, D. J. (1990). The economic effects of intellectual property right infringements. *Journal of Business*, *Vol. 63*, No. 1, 79–90.

Fenby, J. (1983). *Privacy and the Public*. London: Frederick Muller Ltd.

Fitzell, P. B. (1982). *Private Labels: Store Brands and Generic Products*. Westport, Conn.: Avi Publishing Co.

Fletcher, A. L. (1989). Trademark infringement and unfair competition in courts of general jurisdiction. *Trademark Reporter*, *Vol. 79*, 794–882.

Gray, P. (1993, September 20). Adding up the under-skilled. *Time*, p. 64.

Hartford House Ltd. v. Hallmark Cards Inc. CA10 (Colo), 846 F2d 1268–Fed Cts 815, 862; Trade Reg 43, 334, 576, 626 (1986).

Hupman, R. M. (1993). Consumers' perceptions of brand imitators. Unpublished master's thesis, Simon Fraser University, Burnaby, Canada.

Inwood Laboratories Inc. v. Ives Laboratories Inc. U.S., 102 S.Ct. 2182, 72 L.Ed. 2d. 606 (1982).

Kapferer, J. N. (1992). *Strategic Brand Management*. London: Kogan Page.

Leeds, D. (1956). Confusion and consumer psychology. *The Trademark Reporter, Vol. 46*, 1–7.

Lego Group. (1994). *Fair Play*. Billund, Denmark: Lego Group.

Levi Strauss v. Blue Bell Inc., 632 F.2d 817, 9th Cir. (1980).

Levy, S. J., and Rook, D. W. (1981). Brands, trademarks, and the law. In B. M. Enis and K. J. Roering (eds.), *Review of Marketing*. Chicago: American Marketing Association, pp. 185–90.

Mishawaka Rubber and Woolen Mfg. Co. v. S. S. Kresge Co., 316 US 203, 205 53 USPQ 323, 324–25 (1942).

National Hockey League v. PepsiCola Canada Ltd., Supreme Court of British Columbia, No. C902104 (1992, June 2).

Palladino, V. N. (1983). Techniques for ascertaining if there is secondary meaning. *Trademark Reporter, Vol. 73*, 391–404.

Park, C. W., Jaworski, B. J., and MacInnis, D. J. (1986). Strategic brand concept-image management. *Journal of Marketing, 50 (October)*, 135–45.

Simpson, R. N. (1992). The effects of brand imitation on the original brand. Unpublished master's thesis, Simon Fraser University, Burnaby, Canada.

Tauber, E. M. (1988). Brand leverage: Strategy for growth in a cost-control world. *Journal of Advertising Research*, 28 (August/September), 26–30.

Tiffany & Co. v. Boston Club Inc., 231 F. Supp. 836 (D. Mass.) (1964).

Trademarks Act, R.S.C. C T-13, (1985).

Vidal Sassoon Inc. v. Beverly Sassoon and Slim Lines Inc., United States District Court, Central District of California, No. 82–2916 wpm (1982).

Ward, J., Loken, B., Ross, I., and Hasapopoulos, T. (1986). The influence of physical similarity on generalization of affect and attribute perceptions from national brands to private label brands. In T. Shimp et al. (eds.), *American Marketing Educator's Proceedings, Series Number 52*. Chicago: American Marketing Association, pp. 51–56.

Yates, R. A. (1989). *Business Law in Canada*, 2nd edn. Scarborough, Ontario: Prentice Hall.

2

Understanding the Consumer

While the main purpose of this book is to provide information about how trademarks might be similarly perceived, one factor that should not be overlooked is consumer choice behavior. The behavior of consumers is very important in determining their perception of any brand imitation. The various consumer points of shopping behavior, comparison points, intelligence levels, and memory storage are found noted in court cases.

CONSUMER SHOPPING BEHAVIOR

With respect to consumer shopping behavior, Judge Cattanch stated in a case involving brand names and pet food:

The ordinary person buying groceries and other wares off the shelf does not look beyond the brand on the label in distinguishing the origin of the wares he or she is contemplating buying. There is neither the time nor the inclination, during the course of a shopping excursion, to stop and peruse the fine print on the labels, much less appreciate the fine distinctions of meaning that might be taken therefrom. (*Bonus Foods Ltd. v. Essex Packers Limited*, 1946: 20)

Comparison Points

One must not forget that the objects of trademark infringement cases are viewed out of the real purchasing environment. This same judge noted:

In considering the similarity of trademarks it has been held repeatedly that it is not the proper approach to set the marks side by side and to critically analyze them for points of similarities and differences, but rather to determine the matter in a general way as a question of impression. (*Canadian Schenley Distilleries Ltd. v. Canada's Manitoba Distillery Ltd.*, 1975: 5)

It is the point of this chapter to review some of these general aspects of the consumer environment to try to emphasize the consumers' natural decision-making and behavior patterns.

Intelligence Levels

It is sometimes difficult to remember that those who are directly involved in passing-off cases, such as lawyers, brand managers, and judges, are probably more intelligent, more educated, and more involved than most of the consuming public. What appears to be obvious and common sense under scrutiny may not be so for the consumer of average or below average intelligence, education, and involvement. Judge Cattanch may also be quoted with respect to the average person:

It is the probability of the average person endowed with average intelligence acting with ordinary caution being deceived that is the criterion and to measure that probability of confusion the Register of Trademarks or the Judge must assess the normal attitudes and reactions of such persons. (*Canadian Schenley Distilleries Ltd. v. Canada's Manitoba Distillery Ltd.*, 1975: 5)

Memory Storage

The concept of imperfect recollection was also recognized early in the courts by Lord Justice Luxmore (Application by Rysta Ltd. 1943) and quoted by Judge Cattanch. Imperfect recollection emphasizes the natural process of memory and reconstruction of events past seen.

The answer to the question whether the sound of one word resembles too nearly the sound of another so as to bring the former within the limits . . . of the Trade Marks Act . . . must nearly always depend on first impression, for obviously a person who is familiar with both words will neither be deceived nor confused. It is the person who only knows the one word, and has perhaps an imperfect recollection of it, who is likely to be deceived or confused. Little assistance, therefore, is to be obtained from a meticulous comparison of the two words, letter by letter and syllable by syllable, pronounced with clarity expected from a teacher of elocution. (*Canadian Schenley Distilleries Ltd. v. Canada's Manitoba Distillery Ltd.*, 1975: 13)

It is important to keep these points of shopping behavior, comparison points, intelligence levels, and memory storage at the front of one's thoughts while thinking of brand imitation. One must remember that it is the goal of lawyers to do the best job possible for their clients and win the case. Lawyers are very good at clouding the issues and emphasizing the points in favor of their clients. That is what they are paid to do. The consumer behavior issues sometimes get lost in the courtroom. This is a widely practiced tactic of lawyers in defending trademark infringement cases. Lawyers are also known to present incorrect legal rulings, and they may try to get the plaintiff to focus on issues irrelevant to the case (Robin 1992). By doing this the consumer gets lost in the shuffle.

CONSUMER DECISION-MAKING

How consumers make or do not make decisions about the goods and services they purchase or reject in the marketplace is a major field of study in business schools all over the Western world. It is called the study of consumer behavior or buyer behavior. Consumer behavior, as a discipline, evolved when psychologists joined the business faculties of major universities in the 1960s and subsequently the first academic textbooks were written wholly devoted to the subject. Over time, consumer behavior theorists have kept up-to-date in studying how decisions are made in the marketplace. It appears that the consumer is a very adaptive decision-maker, changing his or her behavior to meet the demands of the environment.

This adaptation is largely a result of the change in lifestyles and in the marketplace. It is important to review some history of consumer behavior and relevant constructs to decision-making. It is also important to review the diversity that exists in our consumer base. Too often, one forgets that not all consumers make decisions as we do, or think we do.

The Economist's View

Early models of consumer behavior were rooted in economic theory. In this paradigm, purchasing decisions were thought to be the result of largely rational and conscious economic calculations. Consumers were not only assumed to be aware of all available alternatives in the marketplace, but they were also assumed to be able to rationally rank order the available alternatives by preferences. This is the case of perfect information in the marketplace and unlimited ability of the consumer.

Several problems became apparent in applying these assumptions to actual consumer consumption. First, consumers do not have perfect information in the marketplace. Neither do they have the same information about the existing alternatives and/or the attributes of known alternatives. Instead, each consumer has fragmented knowledge of his or her own set of known alternatives and, as a result, consumers can not always rank order a set of alternatives available to them. In addition, preferences often violate utility theory. Different people prefer different styles, have different tastes, and hence make choices built on preferences of style or image rather than objective information such as price.

These early economic models were not that helpful in understanding the purchase behavior of the consumer. Over time the marketplace became even more diversified and the complexity of purchasing even more apparent. In the 1960s John F. Kennedy became president of the United States and gave the consumer elevated status. In his message to Congress on March 15, 1962, he put forth the Consumer Bill of Rights (1963) as a social contract between business and society. The government was the ultimate guarantor of these rights, which included the right to be informed.

The Consumer as a Problem Solver

As a result of the Kennedy mandate, the government poured millions of dollars into departments whose goal was to make sure that the consumer had access to information. Labels were put on products listing all ingredients. Advertising was regulated, and if it was misleading, corrective advertising was necessary. Information was in great supply to the consumer.

As a result of this environment, consumer behavior researchers started to see the consumer as a "cognitive man." Consumers were now problem solvers. They were receptive to products or services that met their needs. They were thought to search actively for information about the products and services they bought (Newman and Staelin 1972; Asam and Bucklin 1973). Consumers were seen as striving to make the best decisions possible given their limitations.

However, consumer researchers told us that, even though consumers are given information, they often failed to use that information to make decisions. In one choice and evaluation experiment (Scammon 1975), consumers were given objective product information on several brands available in the marketplace. The result of the study showed that their recall of product attributes decreased with increasing information and that consumers felt better about their brand selections with more information but actually made poorer choices. Consumers were limited by the extent of their knowledge about the marketplace and their capacity to store information about the marketplace in short-term memory.

This finding coincided with other research about our ability to use information. In general, we know that humans are able to store a limited amount of information in their short-term memory. This imposes limitations on the amount of information that the individual is able to process and remember in the long run. G. A. Miller's (1956) analyses of cognitive capacity, which showed that seven (plus or minus two) pieces of information were the optimum amount for individual decision-making, held for consumer contexts.

The Consumer as a Simplifier of Information

The overriding conclusion of hundreds of consumer decision-making research studies carried out in the 1970s was that people can only attend to limited information at one point in time (Olshavsky and Granbois 1979). The consumers' skills, habits, reflexes, values, and goals shape the way they search for and use information to make their decisions. Although the consumers' skills are limited, the number of choices available to them increases every day. As a coping mechanism for this overwhelming choice environment, consumers have become "cognitive misers" in the marketplace. They are unable or unwilling to engage in extensive decision-making activities and settle for "satisfactory" decisions.

There is overchoice in the marketplace, and generally people do not spend their discretionary time shopping or making consumer decisions. In addition, the make-up of the work force has also changed, with more married working mothers and single working parents spending their time away from home. Sixty-two percent of families are dual earners and 12 percent of families are headed by single parents ("Two Wage Earners," 1991). While mothers are still mainly in charge of regular family shopping, that shopping is now squeezed into minutes between returning home after work and meal preparation. Their exhausted evenings are spent watching TV and weekends are left for household chores (Cutler 1990). Furthermore, a full third of Americans always feel rushed and harassed (Robinson 1990). The impact of perceived time scarcity causes us to rush in and out of retail establishments at an increasingly faster rate (Berry 1990). Most consumers simply do not take the time to look carefully at the items they buy because they simply do not have the time or the inclination to do so.

It is no wonder that the consumer develops rules of thumb or heuristics to simplify purchase behavior. An in-store study showed that consumers go through almost no brand price comparison behavior (Hoyer 1984). Decision heuristics such as "buy the cheapest," "buy name brands," or "buy what my friend bought" give the consumer a satisfactory choice in the marketplace that supplants an optimal choice. The consumer must use these simple rules because too many goods clutter too many store shelves. For example, the average number of products in supermarkets soared from 13,000 in 1981 to 21,000 in 1987 (Kotkin 1987). Today, major superstores carry over 50,000 items. There are said to be 400 different brands of beer available to the American beer drinker. A new car purchaser might have 300 different types of cars and light trucks, domestic and imported, from which to choose. The market provides overchoice to today's consumer, and the decision-making effort must be simplified.

Level of Involvement

When we compare consumer decisions with concurrent decisions about one's spouse or significant others, children, career, and health, the consumer decisions seem very simple. Furthermore, everyday hassles of traveling on crowded streets or subways cause us to focus on expediting our way home rather than lingering in a supermarket. It is this perspective that consumer decision theorists must keep in mind when examining the importance and effort put into purchase decisions. Kassarjian (1978) put it best when he said the average consumer, who blithely purchases, consumes and discards the product, most likely could not care less. Consumers make the purchase, switch brands, ignore commercials and worry about the important decisions in their lives and not the purchase of toilet paper.

However, when a brand comes before the courts in an issue of trademark infringement, all those party to the case become very involved. Lawyers, judges, manufacturers, marketers, and advertisers are aware of every detail that identifies the brand. They are keenly aware of any differences that exist between the plaintiff's and the defendant's product. It is this close scrutiny that highlights the behavior of being involved. Judges must remember that most consumers never achieve such scrutiny of the products they buy.

The concept of involvement means that the person is motivated to think about the object in question (see Zaichkowsky 1985a and 1986 for detailed information on this topic). When one is highly involved, more importance is attached to the object and more evaluation takes place. Also, one sees more differences among brands, whether the differences are real or imagined. When one has little involvement, little or no arousal exists to motivate the consumer to evaluate the object. Alternatives seem very similar and price becomes a primary differentiating factor (Zaichkowsky 1988). Therefore consumer behavior theorists speak of low-involved consumers, low-involving products, low-involving advertisements, and low-involving purchase decisions. These are usual and frequent conditions of consumers in the marketplace. The implication is that decision-making is minimal, and the most common form of purchase decision is just pure and simple recognition of the product. The legal system must not lose sight of the concept of the low-involved purchaser. Marketers know it well.

It is this difference between the low- and high-involved purchaser that leads to the differences in views of the object. That is
why one gets such varied views on the perception of similarity or
differences among the objects in question. Consumers who are
highly involved with the object under investigation may not be
confused at any time, while those who are low involved may be
easily confused at any time.

Emotional High Involvement. To delineate further the concept of
involvement, marketing researchers and practioners examine a
second dimension of thinking, or feeling. This second dimension
allows for the explanation of why consumers may be highly motivated toward products, yet secure so little hard information about
them. It departs from the original model, which implies that high-
involvement products require a thinking or cognitive orientation
first, whereas low-involvement products are more suited to an
affective or non-informational appeal. The expansion of involvement along an orthogonal continuum from thinking to feeling
allows for a more complex approach that takes into account the
excitment that accompanies certain purchases.

The original classification scheme for products was produced by
Vaughn (1980) for the advertising firm Foote, Cone, and Belding in
Los Angeles. It implies that different marketing strategies, different

Figure 2.1
The Foote, Cone, and Belding Grid for Product Classification

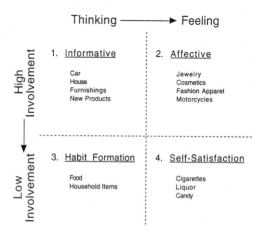

decision-making styles, and different advertising copy are needed for different types of products. The scheme is depicted in Figure 2.1. It proposes that, for a great number of products, the decision process is based on emotion or affect rather than thought or facts. Consumer behavior research in the 1980s was heavily influenced by this model.

In a case on brand imitation of handguns (*Sturm, Ruger & Co. Inc. v. Arcadia Machine & Tool Inc.*, 1988), this theory of emotional involvement was used to explain the likely consumer decision-making process with respect to handguns:

Gun purchasers are more interested or involved than they would be if they were buying a bar of soap, but heightened interest does not necessarily mean that more care is exercised. That only happens when more actual intelligence is brought to bear. It does not happen if the purchaser's heightened interest is more emotional than intellectual. Gun purchasers tend to be emotional. Guns often have psychological attraction for people who buy them. When various complex subliminal factors have convinced a customer to buy a particular gun, he buys it without spending much time finding and reading the objective technical literature. The average customer probably does not exercise a high degree of care in purchasing a gun. (Fletcher 1989: 823)

This testimony also brings forth the notion that involvement and knowledge are not the same thing. They may be correlated, but they predict different avenues to decision-making. Someone who is highly involved with a product is not necessarily an expert on that product. Having knowledge is definitely different from being involved and leads to different types of information seeking and processing (see Zaichkowsky 1985b for more detail).

CONSUMERS ARE NOT ALL ABLE

Along with this concept of purchases commanding so little of the consumers' attention, it is also worthwhile to mention the great number of people who may not make informed decisions because of their lack of ability. Figures vary on the extent of functional illiteracy, but in the United States, approximately 10 percent of the population cannot read or write and roughly 90 million Americans over the age of 16 are basically unfit for literate employment (Gray

1993). In Canada, 24 percent of the adult non-immigrant population is functionally illiterate (Calamai 1987). In France, there are an estimated 8 million illiterates in a population of 56 million (*U.N. Chronicle* 1990). These alarming statistics need explanation for a full understanding of the relevance of illiteracy to brand imitation in the marketplace. Understanding the pervasive aspect of illiteracy underscores the consumer's use of heuristics and cues to make decisions and choices.

What Does Illiteracy Mean?

Measuring literacy has always been controversial because there is no one accepted definition. In 1948, a United Nations commission proposed "the ability to read and write a single message" as a working definition. More recently, literacy was defined as "the information processing skills necessary to use the printed material commonly encountered at work, at home, and in the community" (*Statistics Canada* 1991). In a survey of Canadians, this definition was operationalized as a series of questions. If a respondent scored less than seven on the following ten questions, they were classified as illiterate:

1. Read and understand the right dosage from an ordinary bottle of cough syrup (10 percent cannot).
2. From six road signs, pick out which one warns of a traffic light ahead (13 percent cannot).
3. Figure out the change from $3 if you ordered a soup and sandwich (33 percent cannot).
4. Sign your name in the correct spot on a social insurance card (11 percent cannot).
5. Circle the expiration date on a driver's licence (6 percent cannot).
6. Answer four questions about a meeting arrangement, including the date, time, and people involved (between 15 and 17 percent cannot).
7. Circle the long distance charges on a telephone bill (29 percent cannot). (Calamai 1987)

The results of the survey found that nearly half of the functionally illiterate are 55 or older, even though this group accounts for only 29 percent of the total population. Half of the illiterates say they went to high school and one-third say they graduated. One in twelve who claimed to be a university graduate still tested as functionally illiterate. Illiteracy is higher among men than women, 53.5 percent to 46.5 percent. Illiteracy is also related to occupation. For example, 56 percent of those employed in the pulp and paper industry have a grade four reading level.

A more extensive study was undertaken in the United States by the Educational Testing Service of Princeton, using between thirty-five and forty literacy tests. Examples of questions in these tests were:

1. Signing a social security card on the correct line.
2. Reading the gross pay for the year to date from a pay slip.
3. Calculating the difference between regular and sale prices.

After tabulating the test scores, ETS designated five different grades and projected that 42 million American adults fall within the lowest category and 52 million fill the next lowest rank, still below the level required to perform a moderately demanding job. Seventy-one percent of those in the bottom grade category said they read well or very well, indicating that the illiterate do not know they do not know (Gray 1993).

Therefore great numbers of people may not be able to read labels accurately. They may frequently rely on other cues besides print information to aid their decision-making and choices. This must not be forgotten. It has been an interesting lesson to retailers who developed generic products to target low-income and very price-sensitive consumers. These generic goods had only the contents written on the package as the label. Consequently, most of the low-income target market could not identify what was in the package because they could not read it. The main buyers of these goods were the more affluent, but they did not make up a large enough segment on their own to warrant the continued selling of plain labeled generic products. Most of these generics are now off the shelves of the retailers, making space for more store brands.

Intelligence. Educated and intelligent people who are involved in commerce tend to have a very narrow social world and are not fully aware of the below-average abilities of many consumers. People of one social class rarely interact on a regular basis with members of another social class. Therefore, one often forgets that other people may view things differently. A substantive question is: What intelligence level of the consumer should be used as the standard for evaluating the level of confusion in the marketplace? This question becomes relevant because consumer surveys are relied upon as evidence in determining trademark infringement.

The whole history of consumer research tells us that people who choose to participate in surveys are of higher intelligence and education than those who do not participate. Since most consumer research uses convenience samples, subjects are inherently self-selected, and hence the results are usually biased toward higher education than if a truly random sample were chosen.

The particular product in question has a great deal to do with the sample used in determining confusion. However most products subject to consumer confusion, whether they are frequently purchased brand goods such as cat litter and soft drinks or specialty products such as faucets or guns, are bought by consumers of various intelligence and educational levels. Therefore one must keep in mind that surveys may be biased toward the conservative end of detection of confusion because, on average, those who respond are likely to be more literate, educated, and intelligent than those who do not respond. Actual confusion and potential confusion are likely to play a greater role in consumer choice than we have previously determined, due to the great numbers of consumers who cannot correctly read and interpet package labels.

Immigration of Non-Native-Speaking Consumers

In the United States, the estimated number of legal immigrants in the 1980s was 5.7 million. Canada accepted 1.25 million in the same time period. In 1990 alone, there were 1.5 million immigrants to the United States: 679,000 came from Mexico; 339,000 came from Asia; and 112,000 came from Europe (U.S. Bureau of the Census 1992). The number of illegal aliens in the United States is estimated at around 3.5 million. Ninety percent of these immigrants choose to live in urban centers (Allen and Turner 1988).

While some consumers may rely on visual cues for choice because of illiteracy, other consumers may use the same cues because of language difficulties. The number of legal non-native-speaking residents in our large cities can be casually observed during the selection of juries for the court system. On any given day, count the number, as a percent, of people who ask to be excused from jury duty because they do not speak the language well enough to understand the court proceedings. Some of those asking to be excused have lived in the country for over twenty years. Our large cities are set up so that immigrants can gather together and continue their own language, culture, and religion. This is recognized in public domains, such as hospitals, where the importance of correct communication may be the difference between life and death. A general hospital in Vancouver posts patient instructions in six languages: English, French, Cantonese, Punjabi, Farsi, and Italian.

In many instances immigrants do not see it as necessary to learn the native tongue. That is left for the children to do at school, and then the children are relied upon as interpreters for their parents.

People who do not speak the language purchase goods every day in our stores and supermarkets. The actual number of people who purchase but cannot read the native language can perhaps only be estimated, due to the abundance of illegal immigrants in many countries. Census data from Canada tell us there are approximately 400,000 people who live permanently in that country but speak neither French nor English. This may be a very conservative figure.

Getting a similar statistic about the United States is not as straightforward because the same information is not in the census data. But, on a conservative estimate, if a proportional amount is taken, at least 4 million residents of the United States might not be able to read or write English. It is likely that many of these immigrants are not literate in English and their shopping world may be guided by non-verbal cues such as pictures on the package.

TYPICAL SHOPPING SCENARIOS

Levy and Rook (1981) first interviewed consumers as to their experience with consumer confusion in the marketplace. In general, they found that consumers had three different views with respect to this issue. First, consumers could blame themselves for the mistake. Those who blame themselves admit to being embarrassed that perhaps they were not careful enough in the purchasing environment. Second, some consumers expected brands to be similar from time to time and therefore thought consumers should be aware to make adequate discrimination. Third, some consumers saw the need for legislation to protect companies and perhaps themselves from imitators.

Able, But Other Cues Dominate

The majority of the population that is literate may still make mistakes in the marketplace because other cues, such as symbols, color, and/or shape, supersede any careful decision-making. The mistakes made are often viewed by the consumer as not being serious enough to take any action. Remember, purchasing is viewed by consumers in the context of all the things they must think about during the day.

Real Shopping Experiences. The following situations were relayed by colleagues during discussions over brand confusion. Upon shopping in a drug store, Dr. Wilson decided to buy some vitamins. These vitamins were a major brand, heavily advertised on television. He walked to the vitamin shelf, looked and picked up what he thought were Centrum vitamins. He had bought Centrum before and was well aware of what the vitamins looked like. When he looked closer at the package, he noticed that it was not Centrum but the store brand, which had a design and package color very similar to Centrum's. Instead of returning the store brand to the shelf and picking up the real Centrum vitamins, he put the store brand in the basket and purchased it.

He did not go back and buy what he intended for two reasons. First, he thought, they were only vitamins, and how different could they be? Second, he did not want it to appear that he made a mistake. He thought other people might think he was not that bright for making such a mistake at the point of purchase. This consumer is a full professor who teaches advertising and consumer behavior. Even the experts are consumers from time to time.

The other business colleague tells a story of shopping for Head and Shoulders dandruff shampoo, also in a drug store. Upon examining the brand on the shelf, Professor Smith noticed a similar bottle next to it, picked it up, and examined it. He decided that he wanted to buy the real thing and picked out a bottle to take to the cash register. When the professor arrived home and unpacked his purchases, he discovered that he had purchased the similar bottle rather than the bottle of Head and Shoulders he wanted. He did not take the imitator brand back to the store for an exchange. Professor Smith did not think it was worth his time and he said he felt a little stupid about making such a mistake, especially since he consciously decided not to purchase the imitation.

These types of purchase situations exist every day for most of us. The relative cost of such mistakes might be taken more seriously by consumers if they were aware of the potential damage being done to the original brand.

Hypothetical Shopping Scenario. Consumers do not think about the potential harm to the original manufacturer when they purchase a look-alike brand. The following hypothetical scenario is adapted from Spratling (1973) to illustrate this point for a frequently purchased branded good.

Some months ago, while watching the six o'clock news, the configuration of the container in which the Joy Co. marketed its liquid detergent caught Mr. McKay's attention. He purchased the product because he thought that the shape of the container would eliminate any detergent spills while doing his laundry. Mr. McKay was satisfied with the product and consequently adopted the configuration of the product's container as his identifying symbol for buying the product on subsequent shopping trips. The choice for his purchase was almost automatic, and he did not anticipate the mistake he would make on his next shopping trip.

Mr. McKay wheeled his shopping cart down 2,000 feet of supermarket aisles, past 50,000 different items on the shelves. He paused at the liquid laundry detergent section, and without hesitation, he selected a liquid detergent from among the twelve different brands and seven sizes available. Mr. McKay, like the majority of consumers, purchases goods either consciously or subconsciously by means of symbols—brand names, slogans, background display, color, the shape of the package or container, or even the configuration of the product itself.

Joy Co.'s liquid detergent was chemically similar to its competitors' products. Therefore, its market share was dependent on the degree to which it differentiated its product from other competitors in the product category. Joy chose to identify and distinguish its brand through the shape of its detergent's container. It spent

$150,000 in researching and developing the configuration of the container and another $1,000,000 in advertising it to stimulate demand. The configuration had been successful in attracting purchasers, as well as in providing a recognition symbol for advertisements, which created demand and satisfied repeat purchasers. Joy's efforts resulted in the public preference of millions of consumers like Mr. McKay, and Joy's market share shot from 9 percent to 12 percent, a 33 percent sales increase. In addition, the fact that Joy had been able to effectively differentiate its product mear `hat it faced a less elastic demand curve; it was less affected by competitors' prices. Joy's profits soared.

Ben Co. manufactured industrial soap. Ben Co. realized the value of Joy's container configuration in terms of sales, brand loyalty, and value. Ben decided to enter the consumer market for laundry detergent, hoping to exploit the consumer acceptance of the Joy container. More accurately, Ben hoped to divert some of Joy's customers to its product. Ben spent no money on research or consumer advertising.

Unbeknownst to Mr. McKay, Ben had marketed its product, in a nearly identical copy of Joy's container, shortly before his last shopping trip. He did not realize that he had mistakenly bought Ben's liquid detergent until he examined his purchase at home. As he put the Ben detergent on the shelf next to the old Joy container, he was amazed at the similarity. Mr. McKay felt that he had been deceived.

He is not alone. Market research indicates that in the two months following the introduction of the Ben copy, Joy's sales decreased 16 percent—largely as a result of consumer confusion and brand imitation. Joy is certain sales will continue to decline because previous research indicated that over 60 percent of its customers relied on the distinctive shape of its product's container in making their purchase decisions. Millions of dollars of equity in consumer recognition and good will were appropriated by Ben Co.

This scenario is neither unique nor all that fictional. Companies that copy some identifying aspect of a competitor's brand do not advertise their brand at all. They rely solely on the in-store identification and decision-making of the consumer. This means that consumers may have some idea of the brand they are looking for before entering the store based on previous experience or advertising. The imitation is able to find its way to the consumer's basket because consumers do not have the exact picture of the product stored in memory, only a reasonable image. The concept of imperfect recollection is a real phenomenon.

SUMMARY

When investigating any case of brand confusion in the marketplace, it is important to keep in mind the following aspects of consumer decision-making:

1. Consumers have limited short-term memory and are not able or willing to process all available product information at the time of purchase. They are likely to use simple decision heuristics that allow for a time-efficient choice.

2. Today's consumer suffers from overchoice. There are simply too many options on the marketplace for the consumer to consider rationally. To cope with this environment, consumers make what they believe to be satisfactory but not necessarily optimal choices.

3. Consumers spend less time shopping because they feel rushed and tired from their work days. The combination of mental fatigue and increased time pressure is likely to lead to less concentration or awareness of specific brand attributes when purchasing.

4. Not all consumer purchase decisions are based on rational thinking. Some are based on emotion and affect and may also be independent of the cost of the good.

5. Not all consumers have the ability to fully function in a literate world. If a full 22 percent of the adult non-immigrant population is illiterate, then we might expect one in five consumers to rely heavily on symbols for identification. These people may be more likely than the literate consumer to use cues such as color, shape, and design to select brands. People who are illiterate are less likely to use written information to make their choices.

6. Immigrants often do not speak and cannot read the native tongue. They are perhaps more likely to rely on external product cues for their choice process.

7. Highly intelligent and articulate people may also rely on external cues when they are "low-involved" and hence not motivated to evaluate carefully the product.

8. Consumers who do make mistakes in the marketplace usually do not feel it is worth their time and energy to correct them. They also may not want to admit they purchased something they did not intend to purchase.

These points should be emphasized when trying to understand how the consumer reacts to imitators in the marketplace. Too often judges, lawyers, and other well-educated persons involved in these cases forget that they are not necessarily "average" consumers. They often project their own decision-making patterns to those around them. In addition, well-educated people may not want to admit that they, too, are capable of making mistakes in the marketplace.

REFERENCES

Adult literacy in Canada: Results of a National Study. *Statistics Canada*, Labour and Household Surveys Division. Ottawa: Statistics Canada, 1991.

Allen, J. P., and Turner, E. J. (1988). Immigrants. *American Demographics* (September), 23–27, 59–60.

Asam, E. H. and Bucklin, L. P. (1973). Nutritional labeling for canned goods: A study of consumer response. *Journal of Marketing* (April), 32–37.

Berry, L. L. (1990). Market to the perception. *American Demographics* (February), 32.

Bonus Foods Ltd. v. Essex Packers Limited, 29 F.P.R. 1. (Exch. Ct.) (1946).

Calamai, P. (1987). Broken words, why five million Canadians are illiterate. *A Special Southam Survey* (September).

Canadian Schenley Distilleries Ltd. v. Canada's Manitoba Distillery Ltd., 25 C.P.R. (2d) 1 (F.C. T.D.) (1975).

Cutler, B. (1990). Where does the free time go? *American Demographics* (November), 36–38.

Educational Testing Service. (1993). *Adult Literacy in America*. Princeton, N.J.

Fletcher, A. L. (1989). Trademark infringement and unfair competition in courts of general jurisdiction. *Trademark Reporter*, 79, 794–882.

Gray, P. (1993, September 20). Adding up the under-skilled. *Time*, p. 64.

Hoyer, W. D. (1984). An examination of consumer decision making for a common repeat purchase product. *Journal of Consumer Research* (December), 822–29.

Kassarjian, H. H. (1978). Presidential address, 1977: Anthropomorphism and parsimony. In K. Hunt (ed.), *Advances in Consumer Research, Vol. 5.* Ann Arbor, Mich.: Association for Consumer Research, pp. xiii-xiv.

Kotkin, J. (1987). Selling to the new America. *Inc.* (July), 44–47.

Levy, S. J., and Rook, D. W. (1981). Brands, trademarks, and the law. In B. M. Enis and K. J. Roering (eds.), *Review of Marketing.* Chicago: American Marketing Association, pp. 742–75.

Miller, G. A. (1956). The magical number seven, plus or minus two: Some limits on our capacity for processing information. *Psychological Review, 63,* 81–97.

Newman, J. W., and Staelin, R. (1972). Prepurchase information seeking for new cars and major household appliances. *Journal of Marketing Research* (August), 249–57.

Olshavsky, R. W., and Granbois, D. (1979). Consumer decision making—Fact or fiction? *Journal of Consumer Research* (September), 93–100.

Robin, A. (1992). The defense of a trademark infringement case. *IDEA—The Journal of Law and Technology, Vol. 32,* No. 4, 383–90.

Robinson, J. P. (1990). The time squeeze. *American Demographics* (February), 30–33.

Rysta Ltd. (1943), 60 R.P.C. 87.

Scammon, D. L. (1975). Information load and consumers. *Journal of Consumer Research* (December), 148–55.

Spratling, G. R. (1973). The protectability of package, container, and product configurations. *The Trademark Reporter, Vol. 63,* 117–52.

Sturm, Ruger & Co. Inc. v. Arcadia Machine & Tool Inc. 10 USPQ2d 1522 1527 (CD Calif) (1988).

The Consumer Bill of Rights. In *Consumer Advisory Council, First Report.* Washington, D.C.: U.S. Government Printing Office, 1963.

Two wage earners now are the rule. (1991, October 25). *The Globe and Mail.* Toronto, ONTARIO.

U. N. Chronicle (1990, March). Illiteracy knows no borders. p. 59. New York: United Nations Publications.

U.S. Bureau of the Census. *Statistical Abstract of the United States: 1992,* (112th edn.) Washington, D.C.: U.S. Government Printing Office, 1992.

Vaughn, R. (1980). How advertising works: A planning model. *Journal of Advertising Research, 20* (5):, 27–33.

Zaichkowsky, J. L. (1985a). Measuring the involvement construct. *Journal of Consumer Research,* 12 (December), 341–52.

_____. (1985b). Familiarity: Product use, involvement, or expertise? In E. C. Hirshman and M. B. Holbrook (eds.), *Advances in Consumer*

Research, Vol. XII. Provo, Utah: Association for Consumer Research, pp. 296–99.

———. (1986). Conceptualizing involvement. *Journal of Advertising*, *Vol. 15*, No. 2, 4–14, 34.

———. (1988). Involvement and the price cue. In M. Houston (ed.), *Advances in Consumer Research, Vol. 15*. Provo, Utah: Association for Consumer Research, pp. 323–27.

3

Psychological Principles
Underlying Brand Imitation

Understanding why a company would want to copy aspects of a successful brand requires some review of the relevant literature from psychology. Because consumer behavior is just another aspect of human behavior, marketers have often turned to cognitive and social psychology for an explanation and prediction of consumer behavior in the marketplace. For the concept of brand imitation, learning theory from cognitive psychology is important. A framework for understanding how individuals learn to make choices and discriminations is based on their learning from the environment. Also from cognitive psychology, theories of perception and attention provide an understanding of how objects are perceived or noticed by the consumer.

Social psychology, specifically attitude theory, is important to the understanding of why others would want to associate with owners of successful trademarks. The premise is that positive attitudes can be developed through simple association with well-liked objects, and these positive attitudes can lead to purchase behavior of the associated product, as well as the original product. Most of the theories relevant to brand imitation are very simple.

Figure 3.1
Diagram of the Classical Conditioning Process

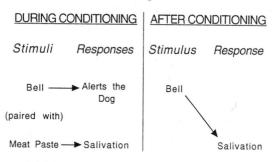

STIMULUS GENERALIZATION

The reason that imitation as a strategy exists may be partly explained by the concept of stimulus generalization. Stimulus generalization means that the individual generalizes from one incident or stimulus object to another similar incident or stimulus object. The phenomenon is rooted in the theory of classical conditioning. This learning theory states that learning depends not only on repetition but also on the ability of individuals to generalize from one object to the next.

Classical Conditioning

Classical conditioning gets its name from the fact that it is the kind of learning originally studied in the "classical" experiments of Ivan P. Pavlov (1849–1936). Pavlov, a Russian psychologist, undertook experiments conditioning dogs to salivate at the sound of a bell rather than at the sight or smell of meat paste. It was the meat paste that elicited legitimate or direct salivation from the dog. To condition the dogs, a neutral stimulus or bell acted as the conditioned stimulus. This bell was paired several times with the meat paste (unconditioned stimulus) presented to the dog. The dog would salivate, which was an unconditioned or natural response. After a while the meat paste was taken away and only the bell was presented to the dog. As a result of the continued pairing, the dog would salivate at the bell even though there was no food accompanying it. This was called a conditioned response. The process is outlined in Figure 3.1.

In Pavlov's case, the dog was conditioned to salivate at the sound of the bell when there was no meat paste present. While the possibility of applying this type of learning to humans might seem outrageous, consider the conditioning that takes place with food. Movie-goers have been bombarded by the smell of popcorn at theaters for decades. The sight and smell thus entices them to purchase popcorn to eat during the movie. It is a learned pairing of movies and popcorn. Now, with the saturation of VCRs in the home, the renting of movies is a weekly occurrence for many households. Coupled with this is the proliferation of sales of microwave popcorn and bagged popcorn. Sales of home-prepared popcorn are at an all-time high, far exceeding sales of popcorn eaten outside the home. People have been conditioned to eat popcorn when they watch a movie. The movie rental, rather than the sight or smell of popcorn, leads to the purchase of popcorn to be eaten when viewing the movie in the consumers' own homes.

According to classical conditioning theorists, learning depends not only on repetition but also on the ability of individuals to generalize. Over time, Pavlov noticed, his dog would salivate not only to the sound of a bell, but to the sound of keys jangling, a buzzer, or even a metronome. These were sounds that only resembled a bell. Thus the animal tended to generalize the conditioned response to stimuli that were different from the original sound of the bell, but somewhat similar to the sound to which it was specifically conditioned. It is this same response to a slightly different stimuli, or stimulus generalization, that facilitates learning or is a key aspect of learning.

Marketing Studies of Stimulus Generalization

Stimulus generalization provides a theory to explain why consumers react similarly to imitations that closely resemble original brands. It also explains why manufacturers of private brands try to make their packaging resemble the national brand leaders (Schiffman and Kanuk 1991). They want the consumer to generalize national brand images to perceptions of store brands.

An academic study of brand imitation dealing with manufacturers of private brands and national brands found that the similarity in physical appearance of originals and imitators was significantly related to consumer perceptions of a common business origin between them (Loken, Ross, and Hinkle 1986). Respondents thought the look-alike brands (national vs. private) were produced at the same manufacturing plant. In addition, the researchers speculated that the physical similarities between brands, such as color and shape, have marketing consequences independent of the product origin perceptions. They felt consumers used the external package cues, such as color, to evaluate the product attributes and to motivate purchase behaviors.

A follow-up study by Ward et al. (1986) provided support for their speculation. In this study, subjects were given various brands of shampoo to evaluate. The results confirmed that different brands with similar packages were rated as similar in quality and perceived performance. The subjects appeared to generalize from the physical appearance of the package to the contents inside the package.

A field experiment, based on the concept of stimulus generalization, provided evidence in a trademark infringement case of breath mints (Miaoulis and D'Amato 1978). The original brand, Tic Tac mints, felt two new competitors (Mighty Mints and Dynamints) had infringed on its trade dress by copying the look of its package and mint. In this study, Mighty Mints and Dynamints were placed for sale in retail outlets in cities where Tic Tac was an established brand, but neither Mighty Mints nor Dynamints was known. Consumers were questioned about their reasons for purchase after buying either the Mighty Mints or Dynamints, but before eating the product. The responses suggested that the consumers purchased the new competing products mainly because of the expectations raised by the physical appearance of the package and the mint. Consumers said these expectations were learned from previous experiences with Tic Tac brand mints.

Some experimental and survey evidence thus suggests that consumers generalize between look-alike brands and may form similar expectations about product attributes and performance based on the external product cues. The concept of stimulus generalization is useful in explaining why a consumer would knowingly purchase a brand imitator.

ATTENTION AND PERCEPTION

Sometimes consumers initially select an imitator brand because they think it is the original brand. They make a mistake or misperceive the actual differences between the original and the imitator. This mistake may be in just the initial identification and may be discovered once the item is in the hand of the consumer. The mistake might also go unnoticed by the consumer until the product is about to be used. In some cases the mistake may be entirely undiscovered by the consumer. In all of these cases, it is not stimulus generalization that is primary, but perception and attention to the object.

The initial step in understanding perception is to understand what kind of things can be perceived at all. For the consumer to use marketing cues in decision-making, the cues first must be *perceived* by the individual. For the cues to be perceived, the individual must first pay attention to them. Attention has two parts, intensity and direction, that sometimes exist in a non-conscious environment. In other words, attention is usually immediate and effortless.

Intensity has to do with the time spent looking at the object. The longer we are exposed to a stimulus, the more likely it is to be perceived. Direction means that the individual must have the stimulus in focus. For example, a disclaimer on an advertisement will likely not be perceived unless the person is led to focus on it. This focusing could be aided by size, color, contrast, and position. These are all important factors in directing attention. The reader must keep in mind that the consumers' main response to marketing communication might be one of disinterest when compared with other aspects of the personal environment. Therefore, attention to marketing communication is likely to be fleeting and superficial, having little intensity and fluttering direction.

Attention to Visual Information

There are several physical properties that direct attention when considered in the context of the visual field. For example, the size of an advertisement can account for over 25% of the variance in readership scores (Troldahl and Jones 1975; Twedt 1952). There is an abundance of evidence to suggest that color increases attention to an advertisement, although many studies of color could be interpreted as supporting the effectiveness of color as a contrast tool. Thus the impact of color depends on the surrounding information (Janiszewski 1991). The manner in which individuals direct their attention to areas in a visual display is sensitive to the characteristics of each piece of information relative to competing information, and to the consumer's goals associated with the processing of the stimulus or information in question. In most cases of product choice, the goals are to recognize and choose, rather than examine and evaluate.

The fleeting aspect of attention is detailed by Janiszewski (1991). The first look at a stimulus (i.e., the first 200 milliseconds) is characterized by a non-fixation, indicative of a holistic analysis of the available information. During this preattentive state, decisions are made about where to look (fixate) first. A decision of where to look involves a comparison of potential benefits associated with an additional fixation to the costs of being "temporarily blind" while engaged in the movement to that area. In many cases, assessing the potential benefits associated with the next fixation may be nothing more than assessing the density or uniqueness of information in that area.

The resulting patterns of looking or direction are highly dependent on the viewer's processing goals. Greater variability can occur when an individual is asked to view a picture for seven different purposes, as seven unique scan patterns will emerge, few of them comparable to those used by others (Janiszewski 1991). In some ways this notion of goals is related to the idea of selective attention. The individual's processing capacity, in the short term, is limited in some central mechanism. This mechanism is associated with consciousness and controlled processing, and it delimits divided attention (Johnson and Dark 1986). Selective attention therefore refers to the differential processing of simultaneous sources of information. Research on early selective attention shows that sensory selection has consistently proved to be more accurate and less effortful than semantic selection.

This was very simply shown by Stroop (1935) in his famous color and word experiments. It is easier for a person to identify the word red when it is in red lettering than in blue lettering. An example applied to marketing would be the identification of a label. If the traditional or original label was blue in color with the brand name in red, the identification would be first of the colors—a sensory cue—and then second of the printed word or semantic cue. An imitator brand using the same colors but a different brand name might easily be misidentified as the first brand due to the superior selection of sensory cues, such as color, over semantic cues such as brand name.

The same may be said for shape as, among the sensory cues by which attention can be guided, spatial cues seem to be especially effective. Stimuli outside the spatial focus of attention undergo little or no semantic processing, and stimulus processing outside the attentional spotlight is restricted mainly to simple physical features (Johnson and Dark 1986). Therefore the individual narrowly focuses attention and does it as simply as possible. These are some of the reasons that consumers mistake or confuse imitators for originals, both initially and after brand choice.

Perception and Weber's Law

Of basic interest in the detection of any stimulus is Weber's Law. It states that in any given kind of perceiving, equal relative (not absolute) differences are perceptible. Weber's Law is a description of the "just noticeable difference" (jnd) or differential threshold level that can be perceived by an individual. This is the minimum difference in a stimulus that will be noticed by the individual or the

Exhibit 3.1
Weber's Law

$$\frac{VI}{I} = K$$

Where:

VI = the smallest increase in stimulus intensity that will be just noticeable to the person (j.n.d.)

I = the intensity of the stimulus before the increase

K = the constant increase or decrease necessary for the stimulus to be noticed minimum difference between stimuli that will be noticed. The quantification and expression of this ratio is shown in Exhibit 3.1.

The main point of Weber's Law is that the ratios, not the absolute difference are important in describing the least perceptible differences in sensory discrimination. The differential threshold varies not only with the sensitivity of the receptor and the type of stimuli, but also with the absolute intensity of the stimuli being compared. The size of the least detectable change or increment in intensity is a function of the initial intensity; that is, the stronger the stimulus, the greater the difference needs to be (Britt 1975).

The use of Weber's Law in the selling of goods is important. Manufacturers and marketers endeavor to determine the relevant just noticeable difference for their products for two reasons: first, so that reductions in product size, increases in product price, or changes in packaging are not readily discernible to the public; and second, so that product improvements are readily discernible to the public (Schiffman and Kanuk 1991). The need to update existing packaging without losing the ready recognition of consumers to the package involves a number of small changes, each carefully designed to fall below the just noticeable difference, so that consumers will not perceive the difference. For example, Ivory Soap, Campbell's Soup, and Betty Crocker Cake Mixes have all gone through many package changes over the years to update their image. Brand imitators may also design their package to be just below the noticeable difference level to the original so that differences are not readily noticed.

Weber's Law can also be heavily influenced by context. For example, with respect to disclaimers, contrast is particularly effective in facilitating perception. Contrasts in size, form, color, and brightness are well known to be effective in altering our just noticeable difference levels. Weber's Law is also important in determining the size of warning labels or disclaimers in the context of advertisements or package sizes. The print and size of the warning or disclaimer must be proportional and relative to its context. The specifics of warning label size and print are detailed in Chapter 5, on avoiding confusion.

PERCEPTIONS MAY BE BIASED

The perception of the existence of brand imitation is often debated. Usually the one accused of imitation denies it, while the accuser is certain of the actual intent to imitate. To understand why these differing viewpoints of the same stimulus are so rooted, further information on the interpretation of perceptions is necessary.

Perceptions Are Selective

Perceptions are best regarded as interpretations made in the light of previous experience. This interpretation occurs unconsciously, and the existence of this step is apt to be denied, for one instinctively places great reliance on the validity and directness of perceptions. However, a lifetime of previous experience must influence what one perceives. Our perceptions, then, are not always valid and they are not the direct appreciation of the environment; they are interpretations of sensory messages, and this has important consequences. For instance, two people will often give different reports when they witness the same scene, not because one is a liar, unobservant, or crazy, but simply because past experiences of the two people are different and their interpretations in the light of their experiences lead to different results. They genuinely have different perceptions of the scene. One need not cease to accept that "seeing is believing," but one comes to realize that seeing is only believing, and beliefs are based on prejudice as well as fact (Barlow and Mollon 1982).

A classic description of this bias of selective perception is found in a case study by Hastrof and Cantril (1954) of a college football game between Dartmouth and Princeton. The authors present an analysis of fans' perceptions of a particular football game between two teams, sitting in the same stadium on the same afternoon, but they saw two different games. The data indicate that there is no such thing as a game existing in its own right that people merely observe. The game exists for a person and is experienced by him or her only insofar as certain happenings have significances in terms of his or her purpose. Out of all the occurrences going on in the environment, people select those that have some significance for them from their own egocentric position in the total scheme of things.

Whatever is perceived is different for different people, whether the object is a football game, a presidential candidate, or a package of crackers. Individuals do not simply react to some stimulus from the environment in a predetermined way. They behave according to what is brought to the occasion, and what each person brings is more or less unique. Therefore perception depends a great deal on personal factors. Past experiences and social interactions may help to form certain expectations that provide categories or alternatives that individuals use in interpreting stimuli. The narrower the individual's experience, the more limited his or her access to alternative possibilities.

Perception and Expectations

The interpretation of the incoming stimulus guided by selective attention is the perception, perceptual organization, or perceptual interpretation of the stimulus. The typical course of perception proceeds from a real world object or event through a medium, to sensory surfaces and receptors, and then to the central nervous system (Cutting 1987). Once the perception hits the central nervous system, inferences from the stimulus may be of two kinds. They may be deductively valid or inductively strong. Perception could be deductive if all premises came from stimulus information, but that is hardly ever the case. Experience, familiarity, or anticipation usually plays a part in passing stimulus information into perceptual objects. Therefore, most perception is inductive, with some premises coming from memory and cognition.

An example of the power of induction in attention and perception to a stimulus object is illustrated by the connection to our sense organs. Whenever our interest in an object is derived from or connected to other interests, our senses adjust to form a close connection in all our behavior and perception. The image in the mind is the attention, and when awaiting a footstep, every stir in the wood is for the hunter his game, and for the fugitive it is his pursuers (Johnson and Dark 1986).

This power of induction to consumer responses can be typified by a personal story. I recall driving to work with a colleague who had just bought a new house and was in the process of preparing his lawn and garden. We drove by a sign that said "Bedding Sale" and he said he wanted to go in and buy some plants. I said I didn't think they sold plants at that store. Then he noticed that it was a furniture store selling mattresses. He was so preoccupied with gardening that the sign "Bedding Sale" for him meant a sale of bedding plants for the garden. He did not initially process the surrounding cues that indicated a furniture store but focused only on the sign that was relevant to him at the time. He was deductively weak and inductively strong in his perceptions.

Illusory Conjunctions. Sometimes people tell us not what they saw but what they constructively have seen. Experiments in cognitive psychology by Treisman and Schmidt (1982) suggest that individual features of objects are separately registered and that in the absence of focused attention, they may be wrongly combined to form illusory conjunctions. That is, people may state that they perceive something that they have not actually seen. The dimensions of color and shape appear to be the most susceptible to separate coding and incorrect reconstruction by consumers.

The implication of these findings in illusory conjunctions suggests that if we see a small, blue triangle, only the labels "blue," "small," and "triangle" are registered. The individual then supplies his or her conscious image with the correct quantity of blue coloring to fill the specified area, regardless of how much color was originally presented. Moreover, the person may use the image to color the area within the specified shape, regardless of whether this matches the shape that was originally blue. The evidence of this study places conscious seeing at a greater remove from the physical stimulus than might intuitively be assumed. We may cognitively rearrange what is actually seen to coincide with what we think we would most likely logically see.

Gestalt

The specific principles underlying perceptual organization are often referred to as Gestalt psychology. Gestalt is a German word that means pattern, configuration, form, or organization and its psychology was founded by Max Wertheimer (1880–1943) and his colleagues K. Koffka and W. Kohler. Gestalt has no direct translation in English, but is commonly defined as "the whole is more than the sum of its parts" (Morgan and King 1966: 26).

The basic premise of Gestalt is that people do not experience the numerous stimuli they select from the environment as separate and discrete sensations. Rather, they tend to organize them into groups and perceive them as unified wholes. Thus, the perceived characteristics of even the simplest stimulus are viewed as a function of the whole to which the stimulus appears to belong (Schiffman and Kanuk 1991). For example, a gray piece of paper is gray only in relation to its background or to something with which it is compared. On a black background, it appears light; against a white background, it appears dark. This type of perceptual organization is called figure and ground. The figure is usually perceived clearly because in comparison to its ground, it appears to be well defined, solid, and in the forefront. The ground is usually perceived as hazy and in the background. The gray will be either figure or ground depending on the context. The eye does not perceive objects in isolation, but rather with their surroundings.

Another example of Gestalt is grouping. Individuals tend to group stimuli automatically so that they form a unified picture or impression. The point of grouping is that patterns or forms of our experience cannot be explained by compounding elements. The perception of stimuli as groups rather than as discrete bits of information facilitates their memory and recall. For example, it is easier to attend to the global features of a triangle than to broken component lines because the Gestalt property of closure makes the global figure perceptually more salient. In the branding case, the consumer may remember the total "look" of the package but may be unable to recall individually small details such as type of lettering, exact hue of color, or the specific picture on the package.

Other types of perceptual organizations of Gestalt that affect our interpretation of the stimulus are:

1. Similarity. Similar elements are seen as belonging to each other more than to other elements equally close but less similar. What the individual perceives from the environment belongs to certain categories. For example, two packages of similar shape and color each seen separately will likely be categorized in the person's memory in the same space. Therefore, the consumer may make a mistake in selecting one over the

other because they are organized together. The two packages are too similar to be categorized separately in the consumer's mind.

2. Proximity. Elements that are physically close are seen as belonging to each other more than to similar elements that are farther away. Proximity can also make things look more alike than they really are.

3. Continuation. Elements are seen as belonging to each other if they appear to be a continuation of the direction of previous elements.

4. Common fate. Elements that move in the same direction are seen as belonging to each other (Robertson, Zielenski, and Ward 1985).

Gestalt psychology explains why objects can be detailed differently but still look the same to the observer. There are many cases of brand imitation where no one feature of the object is the same, but all features are similar. Examples of infringement cases involving Gestalt are found in toys, handguns, and greeting cards. These are detailed in the exhibit in Chapter 4 on cues that cause confusion.

BALANCE THEORY

Balance theory comes from social psychology and the study of attitude formation. It postulates that individuals seek information that is consistent with their needs, interests, and attitudes, and avoid information that is not. This theory provides a rationale for cases involving unauthorized use or association of a successful trademark as in *Bette Midler v. Ford Motor Co.* (1988), where a Bette Midler sound-alike was used in the Ford commercial. The underlying idea of Balance Theory to explain why unauthorized association with a successful brand takes place is that, overall, marketers want customers to have a very positive attitude toward the goods and services they are selling. When consumers have a positive attitude, it is likely that positive behavior in the form of purchases will follow. It is as simple as that.

Getting customers to have a positive attitude toward their product or service is a major task for marketers. While there are several complex, time-consuming, and expensive ways to build positive attitudes based on the creation of good products and images, a very simple way is to associate the good with an object that consumers already have a very positive attitude toward. This implies the use of Balance Theory.

Figure 3.2
Heider's Balance Theory

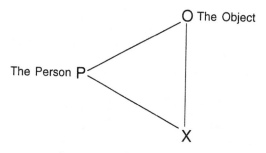

An Object, Person, Attribute,
or Consequence to which the
object is linked

Balance Theory was developed by Fritz Heider in 1946 to explain how individuals cope with their environment. The basic premise is that people seek to balance their cognitive and affective states. In other words, people want their attitudes and feelings to be consistent with their objective thoughts and beliefs. This can be understood by examining Figure 3.2. In the Figure, the link between the person (P) and the attitude object (O) is the attitude in question. The attitude is represented solely by its valence, either positive (+) or negative (-).

The link between O and X represents an association (+) or disassociation (-) between the attitude object and some related object, broadly construed to include people, attributes, or consequences. According to Heider, the valence of the attitude between the person and the first object (P-O) can be predicted on the basis of the valences attached to the person and the second object (P-X) and the links between the two objects (O-X links). Because the individual is motivated to achieve a balanced state, the P-O valence will be determined by the algebraic multiplication of the two valences (see Lutz 1991 for more detail). For example, if Candice Bergen, the movie and television personality, is liked by a majority of consumers, they will hold a positive attitude (+) toward her. When she endorses Sprint Communications, that leads to a positive connection (+) between Candice Bergen and Sprint. The prediction

Figure 3.3
Changing Images and Attitudes

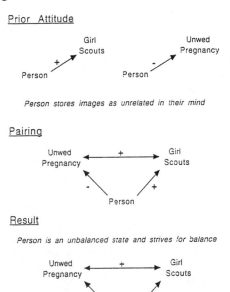

Prior Attitude

Person stores images as unrelated in their mind

Pairing

Result

Person is an unbalanced state and strives for balance

is that the consumer will like Sprint Communications (+) and hence will be motivated to purchase that service. In doing so, the consumer maintains a balanced state.

Balance Theory also explains why successful companies bring lawsuits against other companies that use their property unlawfully or in bad taste. Unauthorized use of a trademark to associate with a lesser object or a negatively perceived object can bring harm to the original through a decrease in the consumers' attitudes toward the original. The negative perception "rubs off" on the original's image. In *Girl Scouts of the United States v. Personality Posters Mfg. Co.* (1969), the Girl Scouts of America tried to enjoin a company that was manufacturing and selling posters of visibly pregnant girls in Girl Scout uniforms, with the headline "Be Prepared." The association of "pure Girl Scouts" (+) with unwed mothers (-) would lead to an unbalanced (-) state, and perhaps harm the reputation of the Girl Scouts (see Figure 3.3). This is due to the pairing of Girl Scouts with unwed mothers by association. The individual has a constant (-) association to unwed mothers. To keep balanced, the previous positive sign to Girl Scouts changes to a negative sign. In this way tension is reduced because the overall state returns to positive (negative x negative = positive).

Case of Balance Theory in Marketing. The unauthorized use of someone else's trademark or trade dress is done to imply an association that should help in building a positive attitude about the infringer's product. Every day, hundreds of authorized endorsements bring profits to companies.

The success of this strategy is demonstrated by the case of Wayne Gretzky for Easton Sports (Cohen 1992). Easton Sports developed an aluminum hockey stick in 1986 and, after an intense six-year struggle, gained a 1 percent market share. In 1991 Easton hired Wayne Gretzky, the Canadian hockey superstar who plays for the Los Angeles Kings, to endorse its product. The 1 percent market share grew to 25 percent over one year. The outstanding success was attributed to Wayne Gretzky's endorsement. This use of Wayne Gretzky to endorse products is not tied to his area of expertise. He also endorses Coca-Cola, Thrifty Car Rental, Ultra Wheels, and Zurich Insurance Co., to name a few. The Zurich Insurance example is interesting as Wayne Gretzky is only a walk-on in the television commercial. His physical appearance in the advertisement is the only endorsement. These firms know that just the simple association with the famous hockey player is enough to boost their sales.

SUMMARY

Theories from psychology help to explain why imitation, as a marketing strategy, is a threat to the selection and perception of the original brand. Consumers generalize expectations from experiences with original brands to similar looking goods and services in the marketplace. Due to fleeting attention and perceptual biases, individuals often make mistakes in their perception of similar but different brands in the marketplace.

In the interests of economizing attentional effort, consumers do three things. First, they narrow their selectivity of attention to things that are somehow essential to the task at hand. For example, in purchasing goods, consumers may focus on price but not on the weight of the package. Hence they may buy a lower priced good but one of poorer value because the package contains less than others. Second, individuals "recode" into simpler form the diversity of events encountered so that their limited attention and memory span can be protected. For example, instead of trying to remember the exact price of a good, consumers may remember only that it was the most expensive of the alternatives available. This may preserve the necessary information and allow the re-creation of any specific information with regard to those alternatives. Finally, individuals deal with the information overload relative to their limited capacities for noticing, registering, and remembering by the use of aids that are designed to lengthen the noticing process. A simple example would be a shopping list, or tearing an advertisement from the paper and bringing it to the store. All of these methods help, but none of them can be fully successful in accurate perception (Bruner 1970).

Objects are often reconstructed from memory, and errors subsequently occur in what people say they saw as opposed to what they actually have seen. This is what Lord Justice Luxmore called "imperfect recollection" in 1943. Individuals may be guided in their visual perceptions by their cognitive expectations. This bias may be inherent and enduring. One of the functions of perceptual judgment is to accentuate the apparent differences in magnitudes between objects that differ in value, provided that the difference in magnitude is associated with the difference in value. When there is little difference in value, objects appear to be similar and we tend to lump them together even more so than they actually are. It is this grouping of similar objects that causes confusion.

The psychological principles of attention and perception guide our identification of objects. Misperception is usually caused by: 1) inattention to parts of the message or product; 2) similarity to other existing products; and/or 3) associations of cues to consumers' expectations of inherent meaning of the cues. By analyzing prior court cases of confusion with the concepts of components of attention and perception, the strength of these cues that consumers use to identify and interpret the object becomes apparent.

Balance Theory from social psychology has little to do with perception or attention per se, but is important to understanding the motives for unauthorized association. The simple association with a likable object leads to two likable objects. Marketers know that simple celebrity endorsement or association with other successful products can increase sales far beyond the benefits inherent in their products. Preventing unauthorized association is extremely important, especially when the connection is made to an object with lesser status than the original.

REFERENCES

Barlow, H. D., and Mollon, J. D. (eds.). (1982). *The Senses*. London: Cambridge University Press.

Bette Midler v. Ford Motor Co., 849 F.2d 460 (9th Cir.) (1988).

Britt, S. H. (1975). How Weber's Law can be applied to marketing. *Business Horizons* (February), 21–29.

Bruner, J. S. (1970). Social psychology and perception. In D. T. Kollat, R. D. Blackwell, and J. F. Engel (Eds.), *Research in Consumer Behavior*. New York: Holt, Rinehart and Winston, pp. 48–60.

Cohen, R. M. (1992). How a celebrity turns your sales around. *Financial Times of Canada, Vol. 10* (September), 8.

Cutting, J. E. (1987). Perception and information. *Annual Review of Psychology, 38*, 61–90.

Girl Scouts of the United States v. Personality Posters Mfg. Co., 304 F. Supp. 1228 (S.D.N.Y.) (1969).

Hastrof, A. H., and Cantril, H. (1954). They saw a game: A case study. *Journal of Abnormal and Social Psychology, 49*, 129–34.

Janiszewski, C. (1991). The relationship between stimulus display and nonconsciously directed attention. Research proposal, College of Business Administration, University of Florida.

Johnson, W. A. and Dark, V. J. (1986). Selective attention. *Annual Review of Psychology, Vol. 37*, 43–75.

Loken, B., Ross, I. and Hinkle, R. L. (1986). Consumer confusion of origin and brand similarity perceptions. *Journal of Public Policy and Marketing, 5*, 195–211.

Lutz, R. J. (1991). The role of attitude theory in marketing. In H. H. Kassarjian and T. S. Robertson (Eds.), *Perspectives in Consumer Behavior*. Englewood Cliffs, N.J.: Prentice Hall, pp. 317–57.

Miaoulis, G., and D'Amato, N. (1978). Consumer confusion and trademark infringement. *Journal of Marketing* (April), 48–55.

Morgan, C. T., and King, R. A. (1966). *Introduction to Psychology*, 3rd edn. New York: McGraw Hill.

Robertson, T. S., Zielenski, J., and Ward, S. (1985). *Consumer Behavior*. Glenview, Ill.: Scott Foresman and Co.

Schiffman, L. G. and Kanuk, L. L. (1991). *Consumer Behavior*, 4th edn. Englewood Cliffs, N.J.: Prentice Hall.

Stroop, J. R. (1935). Studies of interference in serial verbal reactions. *Journal of Experimental Psychology*, *18*, 643–62.

Treisman, A., and Schmidt, H. (1982). Illusory conjunctions in the perception of objects. *Cognitive Psychology*, *14*, 107–41.

Troldahl, V. C., and Jones, R. L. (1975). Predictors of newspaper advertising readership. *Journal of Advertising Research*, *5* (March), 23–27.

Twedt, D. W. (1952). A multiple factor analysis of advertising readership. *Journal of Applied Psychology*, *26* (June), 207–15.

Ward, J., Loken, B., Ross, I., and Hasapopoulos, T. (1986). The influence of physical similarity on generalization of affect and attribute perceptions from national brands to private label brands. In T. Shrimp et al. (eds.), *American Educator's Proceedings, Series No. 52*. Chicago: American Marketing Association, pp. 51–56.

4

Cases of Imitation in the Marketplace

There are literally hundreds, if not thousands, of cases of passing-off to be found in legal libraries. The number of cases seems to be growing exponentially over the years as brand imitation is seen by many to be a very effective means of competition. It is beyond the scope of this book to present a representative sample of all cases brought to the courts. What this chapter does provide are examples of passing-off cases selected with regard to specific cues that may have led consumers to consider two objects as related or mistake one object for another. Passing-off cases found in Oppenheim and Weston (1977) and Oppenheim et al. (1983) were selected as examples of cue identification and categorization. Additional cases were added from court sources and other articles on trademark infringement. The attempt was to find cases that exemplify the importance of brand name, shape, symbols, color, and Gestalt over competing brands, related products, and unrelated product categories. While infringement of competing brands is the most obvious cause of legal action, the documentation of court cases of related or unrelated products that led to consumer confusion is of utmost interest to those wondering about the extension of their brand equity.

NAME SIMILARITY

The importance of brand name in affecting consumer evaluation or choice cannot be overstated (Dodds, Monroe, and Grewal 1991). Brand name is the single most used cue, after price, in determining consumer choice and evaluation. This is probably why most of the confusion in the marketplace is brought on by competitors focusing their confusion tactics on the name they use to label their products. The similarity of name can be between competing brands, between related product categories, or even between unrelated product categories.

Competing Brands

Same Name. It seems that confusion over brand names started the history of passing-off litigation. In *Thomson v. Winchester* (1837), Thomson sold certain medicines of his own preparation under the name "Thomsonian Medicines." Winchester then began to sell inferior medicines under the same name (see Pattishall 1978 for a complete history of early trademark law). In this early case, the court recognized that there was no exclusive right to the name if it had become generic and descriptive of a class of medicines, even though a party may be damaged by the inferiority of the medicines sold under the name. Unfortunately for Thomson, the law paid little attention to the perceptions of the consumer on this issue, or the reputation of Thomson medicines, in deciding that Winchester's actions were not illegal. Consumers and original producers were not protected, and the way was clear for copy artists to benefit from name similarity.

Another example involved the sale of lead pencils by two brothers, *Faber v. Faber* (1867). Originally A. W. Faber created and sold lead pencils with great success. His brother, realizing this success, also started to produce and sell pencils with his name, John H. Faber, stenciled on the pencil. There is no information on the quality level of John Faber's pencils in relation to those of his brother, but that did not seem to matter. The court ruled that John Faber was entitled to use his own name without fraud, despite the fact that it was his brother who created the market for Faber lead pencils.

Another case of identical surnames and identical products is found in *John B. Stetson Co. v. Stephen L. Stetson Co. Ltd.* (1942). John B. Stetson commenced the manufacture of hats in Philadelphia in 1865 and created a national name for quality hats. In 1933, some 65 years later, another unrelated Stetson decided to pursue the hat-making business. One has to wonder if he would have bothered with this business if his name were not Stetson and the public had not known for sixty-five years that the name Stetson was synonymous with hats. The litigation in this case began in 1934 and, despite several orders for disclaimers, the confusion prevailed in the marketplace for over eight years.

Similar Name. A hundred years of experience and some attention to consumer perceptions has changed the way the courts look at companies with the same name selling on the coattails of a previously established successful product. In *Grotrian, Helfferich, and Schulz v. Steinway & Sons* (1975), the competing pianos were clearly labeled "Grotrian-Steinweig" and "Steinway & Sons" respectively, but the court nevertheless found a likelihood of confusion. The court ruled that the issue was not the possibility that a purchaser would buy a Grotrian-Steinweig thinking that it was a Steinway, or that Grotrian had some connection with Steinway and Sons. Rather, the harm to Steinway was the likelihood that a consumer, hearing the Grotrian-Steinweig name and thinking it had some connection with Steinway, would consider it on that basis. The "Grotrian-Steinweig" name therefore would attract attention from potential customers based on the reputation built up by Steinway over many years. Potential Steinway buyers could be misled into an initial interest and might satisfy themselves that the less expensive Grotrian-Steinweig was at least as good, if not better, than a Steinway. Deception and confusion were thus deemed to appropriate the defendant's goodwill. It seems, in this case, the judge was most perceptive to the psychological influences of stimulus generalization.

Another case involving similar brand names in the same market is *American Cyanamid Co. v. United States Rubber Co.* (1966) and the sale of Cygon versus Phygon. These products are pesticides recommended for use on plants such as apple trees, azaleas, and roses. Both brands are agricultural chemicals sold mainly to farmers through the same channels of distribution. Because both brands do exactly the same job, the court concluded that the similar sounding names could easily be mistaken by either the retailer or the consumer. Therefore, American Cyanamid needed to sell its product under a name other than Cygon.

International Cases. Two more cases of the same name for the same product, but with an international focus, are *SCM Corp. v. Langis Foods Limited* (1976), and *Taco Bell Pty. Ltd. v. Taco Company of Australia Inc.* (1981). The first case demonstrates cross-cultural and legal problems in labeling when the trademark laws between Canada and the United States were quite different. In the past, a company in the United States had to use the trademark in the United States before it could apply to register it in the U.S. Patent and Trademark Office. In Canada, however, a trademark application could be filed before using the brand name commercially in Canada. Langis, a Canadian company, had used and registered three trademarks in Canada: Apple Tree, Orange Tree, and Lemon Tree. On the day of registration, SCM started to use Lemon Tree and then subsequently Orange Tree and Lime Tree in the United States on similar products. Three months later, the Canadian company applied to register the trademarks in the United States under an international convention priority right, even though Langis had not yet used the marks in the United States. Six months later, SCM applied to register the same trademarks. The Appeals Court ruled that the names belonged to the Canadian company.

The second case involving cross-cultural registration of the same name involved Taco Bell in Australia. Taco Bell Pty. Ltd. had for several years a restaurant, Taco Bell's Casa, at Bondi, Sydney. It had registered in 1974 in New South Wales, Taco Bell and Taco Casa as business names and commenced negotiations to establish similar restaurants under the same name in other parts of Sydney. Taco Company of Australia Inc. was incorporated in the United States in 1980 for the purpose of establishing Taco Bell restaurants in Australia. It is a wholly owned subsidiary of Pepsico Inc. These restaurants were to be similar to some 1,300 distinctive restaurants operating under the name Taco Bell mainly in the United States. Around November 1980, it was announced that Pepsico Inc. was about to set up a chain of Mexican fast-food restaurants under the name Casa Amiga in Australia. A restaurant in Sydney opened under this name, but its name was soon changed to Taco Bell.

A number of witnesses were called on behalf of the Australian company to prove reputation and to establish deception or a likelihood of deception. The court ruled that the U.S. corporation had no goodwill in Sydney and enjoined it from operating in the area under the name of Taco Bell. Appeals to a higher court were dismissed.

Partial Names. It was also deemed that only partial redundancy cf names was enough to establish confusion for competing brands (*Maidenform Inc. v. Bestform Foundations Inc.* 1969). Maidenform originally had a line of dream bras, including Day Dreams, Dreamliners, and Dream-Aire. Bestform subsequently launched a brand named Teen-Dream. Discussion centered on the common word "dream." The court held that there was likely to be confusion in the consumer's mind.

Advertising Slogans. The expropriation from a brand name to a competing brand's slogan happened in *Big O Tire Dealers v. Goodyear Tire and Rubber* (1977). In the fall of 1973, Big O decided to identify two of its lines of private brand tires as Big O Big Foot 60 and Big O Big Foot 70. These names were placed on the sidewall of the respective tires in raised white letters. In July 1974 Goodyear decided to use the term Big Foot in a nationwide advertising campaign. In this case, the brand name was used by the original tire manufacturer, but the second company took the name to advertise its own brand of the same product. At the time of the trial, Big O's total net worth was approximately $200,000 and Goodyear's net sales totaled more than $5.25 billion. This is a good example of infringement on up-and-coming competition using advertising dollars not available to the smaller company. Upon appeal, the court reduced the damages payable by Goodyear to Big O to just under $5 million.

Other cases involving competing products and similar names include: *LaTouraine Coffee Co. v. Lorraine Coffee Co.* (1946); *American Waltham Watch Co. v. United States Watch Co.* (1899); *World Carpets Inc. v. Dick Littrell's New World Carpets* (1971); *Popular Merchandise Co. v. '21' Club Inc.* (1965), both selling a variety of "21" merchandise; *Harold F. Ritchie Inc. v. Chesebrough-Ponds, Inc.* (1960), Brylcreem versus Valcream hair products; *J.R. Wood & Sons Inc. v. Reese Jewelry Corp.* (1960); and Artcarved versus Artcrest jewelry.

There are many more cases involving confusingly similar, brand names for competing brands.

Related Products

The extension of brand names to other product categories is of recent interest to the marketing discipline (e.g., Keller and Aaker 1992). The value of a good reputable brand name is almost a priceless commodity, as indicated by what firms are willing to pay for brand names. For example, Kraft was purchased for nearly $13 billion, more than 600 percent over its book value, while the sale of the collection of brands under RJR Nabisco group brought in over $25 billion (Aaker 1991).

Another type of brand extensions is licensing. In 1988 Sunkist received $10.3 million in royalties by licensing its name for use as Sunkist Fruit Gums (Ben Myerson Candy), Sunkist orange soda (Cadbury Schweppes), and Sunkist juice drinks (Lipton) (Aaker 1991). Such practices have increased the opportunity for confusion among consumers faced with the same brand names applied to different product categories.

Same Name. A classic case of confusion for related products is *Vidal Sassoon Inc. v. Beverly Sassoon and Slim Lines Inc.* (1982). The infringing product was a skin tightening cream to be used in conjunction with a plastic wrap endorsed by the estranged wife of Vidal Sassoon, the highly successful manufacturer of hair care products. The product, called Slim Lines Body Contour Creme, claimed to reduce inches off the body and was marketed with the name "Beverly Sassoon" on the jar. A consumer survey of 450 target market customers in a mall found that they did not perceive the body contour cream as a Slim Lines product even after careful scrutiny of the package and jar. Instead, the consumers believed that the source of the product was either Beverly Sassoon, "Sassoon," Vidal Sassoon, or Vidal Sassoon Inc. An expert witness advised that the only truly effective way to end the deception would be to remove the photograph and the name of Beverly Sassoon from the package, jar, brochures, and promotional materials.

In *Union Carbide Corp. v. Ever-Ready Inc.* (1976), the related products were batteries and light bulbs. Union Carbide produced and advertised an extensive line of electric batteries, flashlights, and miniature bulbs for automobile and marine use. Since 1966, sales of these goods under the name of Eveready products have been in excess of 100 million dollars a year. In 1969 the defendant commenced importing miniature lamp bulbs having the term "Ever-Ready" stamped on their base. These bulbs were sold in blister packages displaying the name "Ever-Ready" in a four-sided logo, and the package indicated use in high density lamps. Although the products were not exactly the same, the two lines were very closely related. The court originally ruled for the defendant. However, on appeal, the judgment was reversed by a higher court. The higher court gave weight to a consumer survey that showed that 55 to 60 percent of consumers were confused about the source of the products.

In *Sears, Roebuck & Co. v. Allstate Driving School Inc.* (1969), the plaintiff had been selling insurance under the "Allstate" name for years. The defendant was sued after opening Allstate Driving School. The case was won by the defendant, but the ruling was apparently based on the judgment of faulty marketing research. Leading questions were thought not to have elicited unbiased responses from consumers. What seemed to be a clear case of infringement was judged not to be the case, due to other factors.

Unrelated Products

The degree to which two product categories are unrelated may not be obvious, or there may not be agreement on this issue. The degree of relatedness of the two products is perhaps a matter of judgment by the courts; how widely the products are used by the public; and the length of time the products are in use. The question of the consumer's perceptions of relatedness of the product categories is seldom asked in surveys for court cases; rather, the judge is left to decide this issue.

When a manufacturer of vitamins appropriated the name of V-8, the vegetable juice company successfully protected the brand name of V-8, but no research was presented as to the relatedness of vitamins and juice. The reasoning of the court was that consumers might mistakenly infer a relationship between vegetable juice and vitamins. The court judged vitamins and juice to be related product categories. However, in *John Walker*

& *Sons Ltd. v. Modern Shoe Co.* (1954), the two products were scotch whiskey and walking shoes. The Modern Shoe Co. had named a shoe "Johnny Walker." The whiskey distiller felt that the shoe company had infringed on the name of its scotch. The court reasoned that purchasers of shoes would not conclude that the whiskey marketer had started marketing shoes (Stern and Eovaldi 1984).

Same Name. The difficulty for courts in seeing the possibility for consumer confusion with unrelated product categories, despite identical distinctive names and established confusion in the minds of the consumer, is well documented. In *Lego Australia Pty. Ltd. v. Paul's (Merchants) Pty. Ltd.* (1982), the defendant sold irrigation equipment bearing the name "Lego" in Australia. The plaintiff had sold Lego children's building block toys in Australia since 1978, and Lego toys had been marketed in Australia since 1962. Lego toys have been manufactured since 1934 in other countries. The Lego irrigation equipment had been manufactured in Israel since 1929 and distributed in Australia since 1974. The name Lego was adopted by Lego M. Lemelstrich Ltd. independently and apparently without any wrongful intent. It was a combination of the first letters of the names of the founders of the business. The building block name was derived in Denmark in 1934 from the Danish words "leg godt," which mean play well.

A significant factor in the case was that both Legos were made of colorful plastic. Several witnesses said they had assumed that the irrigation equipment was made by the plaintiff because of the name Lego, because it was predominantly plastic, and because companies appear to diversify. Since many households with children own building blocks that are purchased by parents, the issue was that the parents would closely identify the children's toy company with the irrigation equipment company.

A survey conducted by the plaintiff suggested that the name Lego was well known as applied to the Lego toys and was not well known as being applicable to any other products. Therefore it would be possible to find consumers who believed that any product labeled Lego was made by the toy company. The court concluded that companies may and sometimes do expand the range of products they produce. However, that in and of itself cannot warrant a conclusion that a particular company has done so, and even though consumers made unwarranted assumptions or had misconceptions, that was the fault of the consumer, not the company. The judgment was for the defendant.

The same issue, with the same arguments, was brought to court in England (*Lego System A/S v. Lego M. Lemelstrich* 1983). This time the judgment was for the plaintiff despite weaker consumer evidence than found in the Australian case. This ruling shows the overwhelming influence the judge, and also the culture, may have in cases of passing-off.

Perhaps one of the best-known labels is "Big Mac." It is likely that most people will think of a large hamburger in conjunction with these words. However, "Big Mac" was used in advertising a two-liter wine bottle in Australia (*McWilliams Wines Pty. Ltd. v. McDonald's System of Australia Pty. Ltd.*, 1980). The main complaint of McDonald's about the advertisement was the appearance of the words "Big Mac" in letters about three and one-half centimeters in height, extending substantially right across the advertisement immediately below the word "McWilliams," which was in letters about one and a half centimeters in height.

The case made for McDonald's was that the advertisement was likely to mislead the public to believe there was a commercial connection between McWilliams and McDonald's. It was argued that the advertisement might indicate that McDonald's had approved the use by McWilliams of the name "Big Mac" for the promotion of wine and/or that McWilliams and McDonald's had a joint venture to promote the wines in outlets, or that McDonald's intended to sell McWilliams wines in its outlets. The judge ruled that the words "Big Mac" are descriptive. When used by McDonald's, they describe and refer to a particular type of large hamburger. When used by McWilliams, they describe and refer to a particular type of large container of wine. There is confusion with regard to the name, but there can be no confusion between the two types of goods. A consumer purchasing a Big Mac hamburger is unlikely to be handed a Big Mac bottle of wine. It seems the judge agreed that there was confusion, but the confusion was not misleading in the choice of products. McWilliams was cleared of any infringement.

The transfer of established brand names to unrelated product categories is taken very seriously by some companies. A successful restaurant had been operating under the name of Chevy's in Vancouver, Canada, since the early 1980s. In 1990, under threat of legal action by General Motors for infringing on the street name of its Chevrolet automobile, the restaurant changed its name to Bel Air Cafe. This action may seem extreme but, in today's world of global marketing and brand extensions, companies want to be as protective as possible of well-known brand names.

In another international case, American Major League Baseball had to deal with a name that only sounded like another name when pronounced by the Japanese culture. The Japanese patent office ruled in 1978 that the Dodgers name could not be used in Japan because, as pronounced by the Japanese, it sounded too much like "Rogers," a trademark owned by a Japanese candy company. Responding to the league's appeal, a Tokyo court overturned the previous ruling, stating that Japanese consumers could distinguish between the two trademarks (White 1992).

Summary. Protecting one's brand name from use in unrelated product categories serves two purposes. First, if the brand name is used to label an unrelated product by another manufacturer and that product is of inferior quality, the poor image may reflect on the original product. Manufacturers do not want to risk their brand name being attached to inferior products, no matter how far removed from the original product class. Second, protecting one's name in unrelated markets protects future options, because the manufacturer may later want to extend the name to different product categories. Perhaps the more frequently brands extend to unrelated product categories, the more likely courts will grant protection of their trademark.

CONFUSION AND SIMILAR SHAPES

Sometimes consumers identify brands or products not by their brand name but by their shape. Shape can be found in law under the expression of "distinguishing guise." It can be the shape of wares, their containers, their mode of wrapping or packaging wares that is used for the purpose of distinguishing wares or services from others. The shape itself may be desirable or the shape may represent to the customer the quality of the product through identification of the brand. The shape of the article may be protected by a design patent on the aesthetics, but not on the function of the package (Fitzell 1982). Nevertheless, the shape is meaningful to the consumer. Shape may be the initial cue to identification of the desired product. The identification by shape and design takes place in both the consumer and industrial marketplace. If a product obtains commercial success, and this is seen to be related to its design, competitors are quick to copy the design of the product, usually at a lower price.

Manufacturers are eager to seek trademark protection of product shapes or configurations because this form of product differentiation may have four significant anti-competitive effects. First, it may permit the seller to acquire a control over price that he or she could not otherwise maintain. By differentiating the appearance and protecting the distinction, consumers will buy the product even though the quality level is no higher than that of a non-differentiated product. Second, shape aids quick identification of the brand for the consumer, further utilizing non-content cues in the decision-making process. Third, shape adds to the cost of production and marketing by requiring expenditures for differentiation not related to the quality or actual needs of the product. Fourth, entry into an industry is made more expensive because of higher initial losses while the consumer learns to identify the product by a new shape (Minnesota Law Review 1975).

The Product as Shape

In *Sears, Roebuck and Co. v. Stiffel Co.* (1964), the Stiffel Co. secured design and mechanical patents on a pole lamp, a vertical tube with lamp fixtures along the outside. The tube is made so that it will stand upright between the floor and the ceiling of a room. Sears, Roebuck and Co. put a substantially identical lamp on the market that sold at a retail price similar to Stiffel's wholesale price. In this case, any difference consumers perceived between the two brands was likely to be in price. The Sears lamp served the same function and had the same appearance as the Stiffel product. Because furniture has a style but little overt brand labeling, it is unlikely that the average consumer was aware whether the lamp was a genuine Stiffel. The courts decided in favor of Sears, which continued to sell its copycat lamps to the public at a lower price.

A similar decision involving furniture is found in the Australian courts (*Parkdale Custom Built Furniture Pty. Ltd. v. Puxu Pty. Ltd*, 1982). Puxu had manufactured and sold furniture of distinctive design and appearance since 1976. It was advertised widely and had an established reputation. From June 1978, Parkdale manufactured and sold furniture that was substantially the same in design. There was evidence that Parkdale's furniture was inferior in quality and lower in price than Puxu's furniture. The confusion surrounding the origin of the furniture was extensive. Salespeople employed by retailers gave misleading information to buyers. One retail company included an advertisement of Puxu's sofa, thinking it was a photograph of Parkdale's. The evidence of the witnesses showed that the two manufacturers' furniture was so similar that a person could easily interchange them. Despite these facts, the court allowed the copying to continue, citing the previous Sears case as precedent.

The identification of establishments by their distinctive shape or structure is quite common. Because the highways are so crowded, an instantly recognizable symbol of standards and quality can turn travelers and commuters into customers. A uniquely designed building can function as a trademark and convey relatively complex messages in a form of graphic shorthand (Fletcher 1979). This is exemplified in *Fotomat Corp. v. Houck* (1970), where the court held that the overall appearance and design of the plaintiff's building represented "an exercise in inventive skill and creative talent resulting in a building that is attractive and distinctive because of shape, configuration, utilization of colors, design of the roof, and design of the trim" (Oppenheim and Weston 1977: 200). This same identification of the shape as a symbol of the establishment is exemplified by McDonald's golden arches, Tower Pizza, Holiday Inn, and Howard Johnson, to name a few. Just the sight of a pair of golden arches brings pictures of hamburgers and children to mind. Seeing a pair of golden arches that is not McDonald's would be a jarring and confusing experience to most people.

This concept of identification by design and shape is also found in the industrial markets. In *Compco Corp. v. Day-Brite Lighting* (1964), Day-Brite had a design patent on a light reflector with cross-ribs, which apparently gave strength and attractiveness to otherwise unappealing fluorescent light fixtures. People in the trade identified Day-Brite's product by the cross-ribbing. Compco copied Day-Brite's cross-ribbed design so that the fixture was, according to the court, "the same, to the eye of the ordinary observer, and it had the ability to be identified as Day-Brite to the trade" (Oppenheim and Weston 1977: 198).

In this case, the design or shape of the brand served both aesthetic and utilitarian functions. Yet another design, different in regard to the cross-ribs, could serve another brand the same functional needs of the competitor's product. However, the court found that Compco "chose precisely the same design used by Day-Brite and followed it so closely as to make confusion likely" (Oppenheim and Weston 1977: 199). In cases like this, the original idea can be easily copied but given a different execution. A different ribbing pattern would serve the same function but would not likely be confused with the original.

A similar case of shape serving to identify a product but having no particular function is found in water faucets (*Price Pfister v. Mundo Corp. et al.*, 1989). Seven consumer surveys were carried out to identify associations with product shape and to address the issue of brand confusion. In the shape-recognition surveys, respondents were shown a Price Pfister product and two similar handles, and then asked to identify each handle. All faucet bodies were removed and company names and markings were masked. In the likelihood-of-confusion studies, a respondent was shown one of the faucets with its box. The extensive consumer research showed that the copycat brand was likely to be confused with the original brand once the brand name was hidden from view. For some consumers, exposure to the actual brand name did not lessen their identification of that imitator as the original. It appears that the cue of shape can be so powerful that the consumer may continue to confuse a copy with the original, even when the different brand name of the copy is supplied.

An example of protection where the actual brand name may not be known to the customer is found in *Chocolates a la Carte v. Presidential Confections Inc.* (Felsenthal 1992). A Philadelphia jury ruled that a California chocolatier's copyright creations, nautilus shaped sea shells, were original chocolate art-work, and enjoined Presidential Confections from selling its look-alike chocolates.

Summary. It seems that the courts have yet to make up their minds on shape. What seems to be a clear case of infringement for furniture was judged not to be the case for Stiffel and Puxu. Yet the same principles applied to buildings and smaller products, such as chocolates, were judged by the courts to constitute passing-off.

Consumer Packages as Shape

One of the most important package shapes is perfume bottles. The identity of each perfume is closely associated with a distinctively shaped bottle. One of the first cases involving the shape of perfume bottles was *Lucian Lelong Inc. v. George W. Button Corp.* (1943). The plaintiff successfully protected its brand and shape of the bottle. Since then, the design of distinctive perfume bottles contributes to the multi-million dollar perfume business. Some consumers buy the perfume only for the bottle, which is seen as a collection piece.

Specific shape of packaging is an easy way for the consumer to identify products, especially when the color of the packaging is paired with the shape. The following case involving the product category of cat litter shows how similar packaging, despite distinctive brand names, results in brand confusion. In *A & M Pet Products v. Pieces Inc. and Royal K-9* (1989), Pieces began to unfairly compete with A & M by marketing a competing cat litter product with confusingly similar trademark, trade dress, and labeling. In 1987, A & M introduced a new form of cat litter consisting of a sand-like material for use in the usual cat litter box. This sand-like material contained ingredients that made the litter absorb liquid wastes into a well-defined clump, without contaminating the remaining litter in the box. This clumping feature allowed periodic raking to remove only the clumped liquid waste and any solid wastes, leaving clean, uncontaminated litter in the box. Cat owners apparently found the new type of clumping litter desirable because it eliminated much of the odor problem associated with regular cat litter.

To differentiate Ever Clean cat litter from regular cat litter sold by many other companies, A & M decided to market its sand-like clumping litter in standard plastic jug-like containers rather than in bags, which were the industry's standard form of packaging for cat litter products. Hence, A & M differentiated its brand from other brands by the shape of the package. By May 1989, as A & M's sales grew, competitive sand-like, clumping cat litter products were marketed by three competitors. One of these competitors initially sold its product in a plastic jug shaped like the Ever Clean containers. After pressure from A & M's Texas counsel, that competitor agreed to change the type of container it used to avoid confusing purchasers of the product. Of the remaining two competitors, one sold its product in a bag, while the other sold its product in a plastic jug with a different shape than Ever Clean containers. It is acceptable competition to have similar products, but these similar products should be marketed in packages that are distinctively different from the original to minimize consumer confusion.

In 1989, the situation changed when Pieces began selling its brand, Forever Fresh, in the same retail outlets, in identically shaped one-gallon and two-and-one-Half-gallon containers, but at a cheaper price and with a different color label. Although alternative types of packaging were available, Pieces chose packaging very similar to Ever Clean's. Pieces also put very little money into advertising its brand. Only $10,000 to $15,000 was spent launching Forever Fresh, while Ever Clean spent about $300,000. Affidavits from consumers showed that they bought Forever Fresh, mistakenly believing it was Ever Clean. They were so dissatisfied with the product purchased under the belief it was Ever Clean that they decided not to buy Ever Clean again.

The belief that the consumer was purchasing Ever Clean was caused by two factors. First, the salesworkers at the store where the brand was usually purchased told the customer that the same product could now be bought at a lower price. This usually led the customer to purchase one to two cases of the large containers. Second, although upon close inspection the customer may have noticed that the color scheme of the labels was different, the identical shape of the Forever Fresh and Ever Clean containers seems to have been the dominant cue. One customer testified that she assumed the makers of Ever Clean had simply changed the color scheme of their labels. This is a reasonable assumption, because brands do go through face lifts and updating from time to time.

Summary. The shape of the package as well as the shape of the brand are common cues used by consumers to identify brands. Changing the shape may have no impact on the concrete benefits derived from the product, but may be crucial in brand identification. The ease with which packaging may be differentiated is summed up by the court in an early case where the defendant packaged his toothbrushes in a manner similar to the plaintiff's packaging (*Florence Mfg. Co. v. J. C. Dowd & Co.* 1910):

It is so easy for the honest businessman, who wishes to sell his goods upon their merits, to select from the entire material universe, which is before him, symbols, marks, and coverings which by no possibility can cause confusion between his goods and those of competitors, that the courts look with suspicion upon one who in dressing his goods for the market, approaches so near to his successful rival that the public may fail to distinguish between them. (Grubbs 1974: 385)

CONFUSION AND SYMBOLS

Similar symbols may cause confusion in the consumer's identification of the products in the marketplace. A symbol is usually something specifically associated with a name brand. The symbol may be used by the customer to differentiate between the brands. It is usually attached to the object and does not serve any purpose other than identification. In some cases the symbol is very small in relation to the object it represents.

Tags as Symbols

Lightweight luggage was popularized by LeSportsac in the 1980s, and the company identified its product by decorating the luggage with its logo around the zipper areas. K-Mart then brought to the market lightweight bags that carried a distinctive logo "di paris sac" with its own Eiffel Tower design, but all within a background of an elongated ellipse similar to Sportsac's elliptical logo. The judge ruled that this was a case of intentional copying and that K-Mart's logo was not sufficient to overcome possible confusion resulting from the similarity of design and appearance of the competing sport bags.

The court also upheld the trial court's refusal to remove its temporary injunction if K-Mart placed large tags on each bag saying that it was "sold exclusively for K-Mart." The reason that these hang tags, analogous to disclaimers, would not eliminate the likelihood of confusion is that the hang tags would be removable.

Once the tag comes off, the bags are again virtually identical and likelihood of confusion remains.

In *Coach Leatherware Co. Inc. v. Ann Taylor Inc.* (1991), Coach branded its handbags by attaching leather luggage tag-like tags to them by small brass chains. Ann Taylor sold a line of handbags that were very similiar in total appearance to Coach's bags. In addition, Ann Taylor too put a leather tag with a brass chain on the bag. A consumer study showed that 60 percent of the respondents were confused as to the origin of the Ann Taylor handbag. The leather tag acted as a symbol for Coach's products.

A similar example is found in the manufacture of clothing (*Levi Strauss v. Blue Bell*, 1980). Since 1936, Levi Strauss has used a small tab affixed to the exterior of its jeans at the hip pocket to identify them as Levis. The company has also used this tab on other products it manufactures, such as shirts or jean jackets. Wrangler jeans, which had a significantly smaller share of the market, also started to put the same size tab on its casual garments. Wranglers tabs were of different colors, such as red, black, brown, white, olive, yellow, pink, orange, and green. Despite these different colors, a consumer survey showed that Wrangler garments with the tab were identified as Levis. The tab was therefore being used by the customer to identify the brand as Levis, irrespective of its color. This was key evidence in the judgment for Levis.

A symbol can also be part of the packaging. In *Swift and Co.* (1955), the court held that a red and white polka dot banding around the bottom and top of the label of a can of household cleaner was used by the public as a means of product identification. Therefore, competing products could not use the same banding on their brands.

Symbols in Brand Names

The symbol can also be an integral part of the brand name. In *Safeway Stores Inc. v. Stephens* (1967), a comparison of pictures of the stores of the two parties showed that the block-type lettering used in the sign on the Save-Way store (owned by Stephens) was extremely similar to the type of lettering long used by Safeway. The court ruled that Save-Way deliberately failed to avoid confusion, mistake, or deception in this situation (Allison 1978).

In *World Carpets Inc. v. Dick Littrell's New World Carpets* (1971), the plaintiff was the owner of two federally registered trademarks that contain the word "world" along with globe pictures. The defendant used New World Carpets with a globe showing latitudinal and longitudinal lines. Therefore, the globe was the common symbol, whether it was a literal or a representational depiction. The court ruled for the plaintiff and Dick Littrell could no longer use the globe to identify his company.

Symbols in Advertising

Sometimes advertising campaigns are the center of passing-off cases. Advertising always strives to catch the viewer's attention and break through the clutter. It is important that each advertisement has a strong connection to the object it is selling. However, look-alike advertisements are sometimes created. The advertising agency of Chiat/Day/Mojo created an American Express Co. charge card commercial with images of young bathing beauties in a water ballet. The advertisement was pulled immediately after an agency representing European American Bank charged Chiat/Day/Mojo with creative pilfering. The agency had aired an advertisement using an adolescent synchronized swim team in the bank advertisement two and a half years previously. It seems the original advertisement was seen by the Chiat/Day/Mojo group, which unwittingly copied the spot (Goldman 1992).

Slogans as Symbols. Not only do people rely on visual cues for identification, but consumers may also use advertising slogans as a cue that triggers association to the brand name. In *Maidenform Inc. v. Munsingwear Inc.* (1977), debate centered on the rights of both parties to use the slogan "Underneath it all" in conjunction with their respective trade names in their advertising. The defendant, Munsingwear, adopted the name "Vassarette" to identify its Woman's Apparel Division, while Maidenform made use of its corporate name for identification. For many years, the defendant used the words "Underneath it all" in conjunction with the name "Vassarette" as a slogan to promote its women's undergarment products. In June 1977, the defendant learned that the plaintiff intended to use the words "Underneath it all" in conjunction with the words "I'm a Maidenform woman." Therefore, no brand name per se was contested in this case, rather a phrase used to associate the product in the minds of the consumers. The court determined the slogan was entitled to protection and Maidenform was enjoined from further diluting and infringing upon the defendant's trademark.

COLOR

Color is an extremely important cue for identification. The idea that color can be an overwhelming part of the trademark or trade dress is recognized by business, but color is still a very difficult cue to protect. In the case of Fiberglass Pink insulation (*Owens-Corning Fiberglass Corp.*, 1985), the court noted that permitting colors to become marks could result in the degeneration of trademark cases into squabbles over shade confusion. In addition, protecting colors would leave fewer colors for potentially competing products (Fletcher 1991).

The inherent understanding of the role of color by the business person is evident in the marketing community. A Vancouver business wanted to sell tea, mainly to the East Indian community, with a package greatly similar to the leading local brand, Nabob. The name was changed from Nabob to Maharajah, but all other aspects of the package were extremely similar or the same. In fact, the brand imitator (erroneously) copied the exact supermarket scanner bar code from the original brand. In settling this dispute out of court, Nabob proposed that the imitator could keep all aspects of its package the same if it would agree to change the color from the copy-cat red to blue or green. The defendant initially refused. He inherently knew the value of keeping the color the same as the original. The defendant did offer to slightly lighten or darken the color of his package from the original red. Hence, it is easy to see how squabbles over shade might result.

Color is usually accorded trademark protection only upon showing of secondary meaning. Factors determining whether secondary meaning has developed include long use, advertising, sales volume, and identity of a particular source or origin in the minds of the purchasing public. Color protection has been denied unless: 1) it is an integral part of the design; 2) its use clearly distinguishes it from the goods of others; 3) a substantial promotional use has been made of the color; and 4) advertising has established a secondary meaning for the color (Grubbs 1974). Plaintiffs bear the burden of establishing a secondary meaning for their products. The court must decide whether the ordinary user, using due care in the marketplace, would be likely to confuse the products based on color.

Color is an easy means of identification. It takes less effort to identify a brand by its distinct coloring than by any other attribute. For example, the exclusive rights of Coca-Cola in the colors of red and white did not happen overnight, but rather with a hundred years of use and advertising.

Competing Brands

One of the major users of color for identification is the drug industry. Pills without their packages are very difficult to label, so color combinations are used as surrogates for labels. The color coding can be a life or death matter. The colors are functional to patients as well as doctors, nurses, and hospitals. This functional aspect of color was germane to *Inwood Laboratories Inc. v. Ives Laboratories Inc.* (1982). In 1955 Ives received a patent on the drug cyclandelate. After Ives' patent expired, Inwood copied the appearance of the original capsules, selling cyclandelate in 200mg and 400mg capsules in colors identical to those selected by Ives. The Supreme Court ruled that specific color combinations helped avoid confusion among chemically different drugs by those responsible for dispensing them. The liberal definition of secondary meaning referred to the product rather than the individual brand. This leads to an interesting scenario, as the same drug with different colors might have an extremely difficult time being accepted on the marketplace.

A similar outcome centering over color and drugs is found in *Norwich Pharmacal Co. v. Sterling Drug Inc.* (1960). Norwich sold a pink-colored stomach remedy, Pepto-Bismol, in clear glass bottles, thus presenting a pink trade dress. The defendant also sold a pink stomach remedy called Pepsamar in clear glass bottles. Both products were pink due to the addition of food coloring. Other aspects of the defendant's packaging were different, such as the shape of the bottle, the color and size of the label, and the size of lettering on the label. The judgment was for Sterling, which showed that there were thirty-three other pink stomach remedies on the market (Schultz 1977).

Secondary Meaning. A case of color and secondary meaning is the Yellow Pages telephone directory (*Southwestern Bell Telephone Co. v. Nationwide Directory Service Inc.*, 1974). The phrase "yellow pages" appears with the yellow pages symbol on the front cover and the yellow-colored pages in the advertising section. The court found the yellow pages format had achieved trademark status and granted a permanent injunction against the other "Yellow Pages." In recent years competitors have tried to come into the market as "Pink Pages." Although there was no confusion, they were driven out of business by very aggressive and competitive advertising for Yellow Pages.

MARS Inc., the large candy company, went to court against Cool Chocolate Inc. to protect itself from the widespread rumor that green M & M's are powerful aphrodisiacs. The rumor largely circulated among 15- to 30 year olds, and is said to have originated years ago with reports that the rock group Van Halen demanded that green M & M's be provided at every concert (Hwang 1992). Cool Chocolate Inc. sold its green product as an alleged aphrodisiac, and Mars was seeking a permanent injunction and damages.

Related Products

The overriding use of color for brand identification is found in *Eastman Kodak Co. v. Fotomat Corp.* (1969). Fotomat simulated the trade dress of Eastman Kodak Co. by using a yellow color for its roof and yellow, red, and black colors on signs. In addition, Fotomat used large signs reading "Kodak Film" without clear identification of Fotomat itself. The court decided the likely result was that customers assumed Fotomat was associated with Kodak. The court thus ruled for Eastman Kodak Co.

Unrelated Products

Color was a secondary attribute contributing to confusion in *Church & Dwight Co. Inc. v. Helene Curtis et al.* (1977). Helene Curtis brought onto the market a new brand of deodorant called "Arm and Arm" using the colors of yellow and red to identify its package. In previous years, Church and Dwight had sold Arm and Hammer baking soda in yellow and red packaging. Thus it was argued that the consumer might be misled to believe that the same company was now selling deodorant as well as baking soda. After winning its court case against Helene Curtis, Church and Dwight subsequently brought Arm and Hammer deodorant to the marketplace.

SIMILAR GROUPING OR GESTALT

People do not perceive situations or events as made up of many discrete elements, but rather as dynamic wholes. This emphasis on perceiving the environment as a whole that is more than the sum of its parts is known as Gestalt, from the German word for shape or form. A core idea in this perspective is that people tend spontaneously to group and categorize objects.

The idea of Gestalt is very useful, especially in our consideration that people can absorb only a limited amount of the stimulation they are bombarded with every minute. When individuals need to retrieve previous images from memory, they cannot get it all back in one complete accurate picture. Any analyses of product/brand perception must start out by acknowledging our limited processing abilities. Remember, consumers are cognitive misers who try to cut corners and save effort. Consumers do not try to perceive or remember all possible bits of product information; they do only what is necessary to get a clear impression of what is going on. People take in information selectively, then organize it into a meaningful Gestalt that makes sense of the selective information. This is why products with the same trade dress may be confused with one another, despite very different brand names.

Competing Brands

The importance of Gestalt was realized very early by the courts (*Fischer v. Blank*, 1893). In 1888, Benedickt Fischer began marketing its Russian Caravan tea in oblong boxes with black wrappers containing the following features: 1) the name "Black Package Tea"; 2) three scenes in white, one depicting a caravan crossing a desert, and the other two representing snow; 3) a silver label on which the Russian words for "Russian Caravan Tea" were printed; and 4) a white, diamond-shaped label bearing the plaintiff's business name.

Some time later, Berthold Blank began to sell the same type of tea in boxes of the same size and shape as the plaintiff's, also in black wrappers, and also called "Black Package Tea." This package also bore scenes and labels substantially identical to the distinctive designs of the original. The only difference was in the words printed on the labels. On the white label, the name Blank replaced the name Fischer; and on the silver label, the Russian printing used different words. The court drew the following inference:

[T]he object and the intent of the defendant was to put up his tea in packages so similar to those of the plaintiffs that they would be mistaken for the packages of the latter, and yet that the differences upon the wrappers should be such that the plaintiffs would not be able to maintain an action to restrain the defendant from selling his tea in such packages. (Schultz 1977: 660)

The inevitability of purchaser confusion was noted as follows:

The prospective purchasers are for the most part foreigners, many of whom are illiterate, . . . and the tea is sold in many cases in dark shops and cellars, where there is not sufficient light to enable a person to distinguish between packages which bear a general resemblance to one another. . . . The differences between the packages can be seen upon close inspection, but without such inspection the general appearance of the defendant's packages is so nearly the same as that of the plaintiffs' packages that any person, whether illiterate or not, if making a purchase in a place where the light was not good, would readily mistake the packages. (Schultz 1977: 660–61)

Stressing the limited significance of individual packaging elements when viewed in an isolated context, the court conceded:

[T]here is no single point of resemblance or imitation, which would of itself be regarded as adequate grounds for the grant of equitable relief. Form alone would not be sufficient; nor size; nor color; nor the general decoration of the panels; nor the disks of the same size and color arranged the same way; nor a label of the same shape and color attached to the same part; nor the use of the same name to designate the kind of quality of the product. Each one of these distinguishing features might be separately used and no harm result. (Schultz 1977: 661)

It is clear that it is the combination of features that is important.

Because Gestalt refers to the overall look of the item, there may be many distinctive features that are grouped together to give an overall impression of the object. For example, in *Harold F. Ritchie Inc. v. Chesebrough-Ponds Inc.* (1960), two men's hair care products were sold under the similar names of Brylcreem and Valcream. However, it was not only these similar names that led to confusion. The brands were similarly presented with respect to their design and general appearance, containers, tubes, price, size, perfume, and other non-functional aspects.

Other products may be sold with distinctly different names, but many of the other features are so similar that the distinctive names are ignored. This has happened several times in the publishing business. In *Dell Publishing Company v. Norwood Publishing Company* (1934), Dell had developed a distinctive magazine called *Film Fun*. Subsequently Norwood published *Movie Humor*. Despite the different names, the visual package experience was similar. The court noted that the method of printing the price, the descriptive letters on the cover, and the exclamation point were elements that undoubtedly tended to confuse the consumer. The possibilities of confusion were aggravated by the identitical format of the two publications and their equal number of pages. To prevent confusion, Norwood was instructed to change its type of lettering, placement of price, and slogans (Schultz 1977).

The same problem and judgment were found forty years later in *Creem Magazines Inc. v. Modern Day Periodicals Inc.* (1976) involving two rock music magazines. Despite the differences in the names, "Creem" and "Rock," the court found their respective covers too similar. Having very different names is not enough to differentiate the similar-looking products in the same marketplace.

The similar look is not confined to product categories. In *Maternally Yours Inc. v. Your Maternity Shop* (1956), the two retail establishments had similar signs, labels, boxes, advertising slogans, and telephone listings. The total visual image was deemed more important in confusing the two establishments than any one aspect.

EXHIBIT 4.1
Distinctive Features Establishing Gestalt

Blue Mountain Greeting Cards

1) A two-fold card containing poetry on the first and third page.

2) Unprinted surfaces on the inside three panels.

3) A deckle edge on the right side of the first page.

4) A rough edge stripe of colour or wide stripe on the outside of the deckle edge of the first page.

5) A high quality, uncoated and textured art paper for the cards.

6) Florescent ink for some of the colours printed on the cards.

7) Length of poetry, written in free verse, typically with a personal message.

8) Appearance of hand-lettered calligraphy on the first and third page with the first letter of the words sometimes enlarged.

9) The illustration on the cards "wraps around" the card and is spread over three pages including the back of the card.

10) The actual style and 'look' of the cards is characterized by backgrounds of soft colours done with airbrush blend or light watercolour strokes; they usually depict simple contrasting foreground scenes superimposed in the background.

Ruger Guns

1) Shape and angle of the grip to the barrel.

2) Shape and slant of the bottom of the grip.

3) Shape of the external portions of the magazine and the location of the magazine release.

4) Slant of the back of the bolt and receiver.

5) Shape of the bolt ears used for pulling the bolt back in preparation for firing.

6) The shape and location of the ejection port.

7) The location and style of the safety and bolt stop.

8) The angle and shape of the front portion of the grip frame.

9) The shape of the trigger and trigger guard.

10) The amount of the barrel which is left exposed.

Care Bears

1) Pastel colouration.

2) An inverted triangular "jowly: shaped head.

3) Heart-shaped paws.

4) Pear-shaped body.

5) An oval-shaped abdominal area.

6) A heart-shaped nose.

7) A tuft of hair atop the head.

8) A white plush abdominal area.

9) Tummy graphics.

A similar concern about Gestalt confusion is found in *Palace Station Inc. v. Ramada Station Inc.* (1988). Ramada was accused of using a railroad station theme confusingly similar to Palace Station's old-time railroad station motif in the advertising, promotion, development, and operation of its Laughlin, Nevada, hotel-casino. The judge ruled that the exterior and interior thematic design of a hotel-casino serves no engineering or scientific purpose. It did not make the facility safer, more energy efficient, less costly to construct or maintain, nor did it enable the patron to gamble more conveniently or more effectively. Therefore, the look or Gestalt of the infringing structure as a railroad station had to be changed.

The pervasive but elusive aspect of Gestalt is found in *American Greetings Corp. v. Dan-Dee Imports Inc.* (1985); *Sturm, Ruger & Co. Inc. v. Arcadia Machine & Tool Inc.* (1988); and *Hartford House Ltd. v. Hallmark Cards Inc.* (1986). A detailed description of the original brands is given in Exhibit 4.1. Confusion is pervasive but elusive because there is no one or overriding aspect that is important in these cases. In the first case, plush toys were sold under the name of "Care Bears," as against "Good Time Gang." The competitors' plush, stuffed toy bears and other animals were likely to be confused with the manufacturers' pre-existing plush, pastel-colored teddy bears. The infringing bears had various graphic symbols placed on the white background of their bellies. The first manufacturer had used the same device to develop a strong product appearance with a clear secondary meaning. The competitor knowingly copied the overall appearance of the first manufacturer's bears. The overall appearance of the two lines of products was so similar that a manufacturers' survey showed that 42 percent of customers associated the competitor's products in some way with those of the original manufacturer. Thus Dan-Dee Imports was enjoined from further selling its look-alike goods.

In *Sturm, Ruger & Co. Inc. v. Arcadia Machine & Tool Inc.* (1988) the basis for confusion was between two brands of handguns. The similarities between the two guns were extensive. Photographs and drawings of the AMT Lightning pistols appearing in gun magazine articles and advertisements were misidentified as Rugers in the accompanying printed explanations and advertising copy. A market research study was conducted to measure the distinctiveness of the Ruger Mark II within the product category and the extent of confusion between the AMT and Ruger pistols. A sample of 311 people who had purchased a handgun in the last five years was divided into two groups, shown pictures of five pistols, and asked to identify them. One group had the Ruger in the five pictures and the other group had the AMT in the pictures. On an unaided basis, 46 percent of those shown the photograph of the Ruger pistol correctly identified it as being a Ruger. However, 39 percent of handgun buyers identified the AMT as the Ruger, while 3 percent correctly identified the AMT. Ruger won its case.

A particularly aggressive instance of the imitation can be found in *Hartford House v. Hallmark Cards Inc.* (1986). Blue Mountain cards are unique in the industry because they have a definite distinctive style that has been developed over fifteen years. In March 1985 Hallmark's CEO came to visit Blue Mountain to negotiate a joint venture but Blue Mountain declined. In September 1985, Hallmark conducted market research to determine the effectiveness of its copycat product, Personal Touch, as compared with the Blue Mountain product. The report advised that the sales force could use the information to reduce or eliminate Blue Mountain Art displays and insert its own Personal Touch displays. In April 1986, the owner of Blue Mountain testified that as she went to straighten an in-store display of her cards and turned over a card, to her shock and disbelief she discovered that it was an imitation bearing the Hallmark name. The copy was so convincing that it fooled even the owner of the original company. The request for damages and costs from Hallmark was $50 million. It took Blue Mountain years to develop its cards' style and look; Hallmark tried to do it in a matter of months. The court ruled that Hallmark must select and incorporate alternative features to avoid the potential for confusion. It was told to alter and rearrange the features of its cards in such a way as to produce a card different from Blue Mountain's.

Sometimes the roles of David and Goliath are reversed. Ruger guns and Care Bears were originally created by established companies, and lesser companies tried to piggy-back on the coattails of their success. However, the Blue Mountain greeting card case is an example of a "little guy" who created and built a successful business only to have an established multi-million dollar company, Hallmark, try to reduce or eliminate it.

In these cases it was determined that the competitor intentionally and knowingly copied the overall appearance of the original product. The look was so complete for the Hallmark greeting cards that the creator of the original Blue Mountain cards could not tell the difference. The important point well known to Gestalt psychologists is that there need not be one distinctive feature in isolation that creates the similar grouping of perception. It is the integration of all the features taken as a whole.

Gestalt of Advertising

Courts have recently begun deciding advertising copyright infringement cases by comparing the "look and feel" of the commercials instead of single elements (Goldman 1992). The idea behind using the whole advertisement is that one would have had to see the original in order to create the infringing advertisement. This is certainly a step forward but, unfortunately, sometimes this "look and feel" is taken apart by focusing on the different individual small elements.

Sometimes it is difficult for judges to understand Gestalt. In the *National Hockey League v. Pepsi-Cola Canada Ltd.* (1992), market research showed that 68 percent of viewers of the advertisement in question believed the NHL to have sponsored or be associated with Pepsi's promotion and advertising. This belief might have been largely due to the incorporation of several factors common to the NHL in Pepsi's advertising: the Stanley Cup Playoffs, look-alike team uniforms, and hockey commentators. Yet the judge ruled for Pepsi based on his own impressions of the ads viewed in the close scrutiny of the courtroom (McKelvey 1993).

IMPLIED ASSOCIATION

Endorsement by or simple association of a product or brand with a celebrity or well-liked image can transfer popularity to the product in the minds of the consumer. Under the simple rules of Heider's Balance Theory (see Chapter 3 for a detailed discussion) the individual seeks to maintain a steady state among his or her relationships. If the consumer likes a certain pop star, say Madonna, and Madonna endorses Coca-Cola, then the consumer should like Coca-Cola to maintain the state of balance. It is the association, in the minds of the consumer, that is important.

Knowing how important association is to sales leads manufacturers to use association without consent. This use without consent creates problems in the marketplace. The association may be made using the Gestalt of the person (e.g., *Motschenbacher v. R. J. Reynolds Tobacco Co.*, 1974) or a specific symbol (e.g., *Bette Midler v. Ford Motor Co.*, 1988).

In an R. J. Reynolds television commercial for Winston cigarettes, the photograph of a famous professional racing driver's car was used without his permission. Although the number on the car was changed and a wing-like device known as a spoiler was attached to the car, other features were not disguised. The car still had white pinpointing, an oval medallion, and a solid red coloring. The driver, Motschenbacher, was in the car but his features were not visible. On viewing the commercial, some people correctly inferred that the car was his and that he was in the car and was therefore endorsing the product. The lower court found in favor of R. J. Reynolds. However, on appeal, the higher court overturned the judgment and sent it back to the lower court. The appeals court ruled that it was irrelevant that Motschenbacher could not be identified in the advertisement. The advertisement suggested he was, by emphasizing distinctive signs or symbols associated with him.

In a similar case, Bette Midler successfully sued Ford Motor Co. (1988) and its advertising agency, Young and Rubicam Inc., for $400,000 over an advertisement for Ford Lincoln Mercury that used a "sound-alike" singer. Neither the name nor the picture of Bette Midler was used in the commercial. The advertising agency had originally approached Ms. Midler's manager, who flatly refused the offer. Undeterred, the advertising agency recruited one of Midler's back-up singers with instructions to sound as much like Midler as possible. The district court described the defendant's conduct as that of "of the average thief," saying it had decided, "If we can't buy it, we'll take it." The cue in this case was a very distinctive voice, expertly copied.

The association that leads to liking does not have to be a person; it can be an image that is falsely implied. In *Narhex Australia Pty. Ltd. v. Sunspot Products Pty. Ltd.* (1990), Narhex misleadingly represented a connection between its Japanese manufactured skin care products and France by the impression conveyed by the packaging or labeling of the products. This French image was created by the use of the word "Paris" and the phrase "creme des yeux pour les rides a' l'élastine," which was on the front and sides of the package. Instructions were written in French and English inside the package and reference was made to "laboratoire de Narhex Paris-France" and to the work of French scientists at the University of Paris.

In fact, Narhex elastin was manufactured in Japan for Narhex Australia Pty. Limited and was not distributed in France. The court considered that the color and labeling on the packaging combined to convey the impression of a connection with France. The justice in this case acknowledged the importance of the package's image in its association to France.

A reference to a French origin for a product or an indication of its acceptance by French people, especially Parisians, serves greatly to enhance consumer expectations as to its efficacy and to increase consumer willingness to pay a higher price for it.

Association and Defamation of Character

Companies sometimes make money by selling their name to other manufacturers. This licensing of brand names is big business. For example, in 1988 Sunkist received $10.3 million in royalties by extending its name for use as Sunkist Fruit Gums (Ben Myerson Candy), Sunkist orange soda (Cadbury Schweppes), and Sunkist juice drinks (Lipton) (Aaker 1991). In these instances, the trademark does not serve as an indication of source, but rather of quality. Consumers may have come to expect a specific level of quality through their prior experience with the original product bearing the brand and then may transfer that expectation to the second product. This is why cases dealing with sponsorship or even association may serve as the basis for infringement. If a second firm implies that it is associated with a successful brand, any consumer dissatisfaction with its product or service will be at the expense of the original's reputation and good will, even when the two parties are not in direct competition.

The reasoning behind keeping one's product away from unwanted association can be explained by the Balance Theory of attitudes. Just as companies want to associate with positive images to form positive attitudes and hence lead to purchase, negative associations lead to negative attitudes and images and avoidance of the product. In *General Foods Co. v. Gag Foods Co.*, Gag Foods produced and sold a product called "Roadkill Helper" from a distance, looked identical to the "Hamburger Helper" product by General Mills (Gibson 1993). This image of using a product to eat the inedible is not very appetizing.

Recognition of the wide-reaching nature of trademarks was made by the courts in 1934.

His mark is this authentic seal; by it he vouches for the goods which bear it; it carries his name for good or ill. If another uses it, he borrows the owner's reputation, whose quality no longer lies within his own control. This is an injury, even though the borrower does not tarnish it, or divert any sales by its use; for a reputation, like a face, is the symbol of its possessor and creator, and another can use it only as a mask. (Denicola 1982: 164)

The association or connection does not have to be direct. The simple fact that the sight of a familiar trademark will call to mind the trademark owner is enough to cause infringement. A legal action in these cases is likely to be brought because the association dilutes or harms the image and reputation of the first party. The chief value of a trademark is its selling power, which depends not only on the quality of the goods or services sold under the mark, but on the impression or image created by the mark itself.

Injury to business reputation has both successes and failures in the courtroom. The Dallas Cowboys Cheerleaders have been successful in enjoining a pornographic movie featuring an actress occasionally clad in a cheerleader's uniform (*Dallas Cowboys Cheerleaders Inc. v. Pussycat Cinema Ltd.*, 1979) and a poster depicting a group of past members wearing only a portion of their former attire (*Dallas Cowboys Cheerleaders Inc. v. Scoreboard Posters Inc.*, 1979). In the first case, the central character of the pornographic film is selected to become a Texas Cowgirl, a name sometimes used for the cheerleaders. To raise money for the trip to Dallas, the heroine engages in a variety of sexual activities, sometimes attired in a uniform strikingly similar to that worn by the actual Dallas Cowboys Cheerleaders. The court stated, "It is hard to believe that anyone who had seen the sexually depraved film could ever thereafter disassociate it from the Dallas cheerleaders" (Denicola 1982: 206).

The judicial concern here is the unwelcome association rather than the threat of confusion. The owner of the mark wants to prevent the appearance of his mark in an unwholesome or inappropriate environment. In this vein, General Electric was granted an injunction against the use of "Genital Electric" on T-shirts and briefs (*General Electric Co. v. Alumpa Coal Co.*, 1979). In another case, the Pillsbury trade characters Poppin Fresh and Poppie Fresh were depicted in an adult newspaper engaged in sexual activities incompatible with the wholesome image sought by their owner (*Pillsbury Co. v. Milky Way Prods. Inc.*, 1981).

Just placing the original mark in an unflattering context can be grounds for relief. A decision enjoined the use of a well-known "Enjoy Coca-Cola" design on a poster featuring a facsimile of the symbol, but advocating instead, "Enjoy Cocaine" (*Coca-Cola Co. v. Gemini Rising Inc.*, 1972). Anheuser-Busch successfully invoked the traditional confusion standard to prevent the use of its slogan "Where there's life—there's Bud," by a manufacturer of insecticide who had adapted the phrase to his own purposes by substituting the word "Bugs" for "Bud" (*Chemical Corp. of America v. Anheuser-Busch Inc.*, 1963).

Undermining the positive image can even be a case for diminishing distinctiveness, uniqueness, effectiveness, or prestigious connotations. The court held that the use of the name "Tiffany's" by a Boston night club harmed the New York jeweler's mark and characterized the nature of the injury as a risk of erosion on the public's identification (*Tiffany & Co. v. Boston Club Inc.*, 1964).

Failures to determine injury with direct association can also be found in the legal system. A New York State court declined to grant an injunction to the University of Notre Dame prohibiting the use of its name and symbols in a comic film that parodied its football program (*University of Notre Dame Du Lac v. Twentieth Century-Fox Film Corp.*, 1965). Even the Girl Scouts of America have found themselves in court. They were unable to prevent the use of their trademarks on a poster depicting a pregnant scout and the motto, "Be Prepared" (*Girl Scouts of the United States v. Personality Posters Mfg. Co.*, 1969).

SUMMARY

The imitation of brand name, shape, symbol, color, and trade dress in competing brands, related products, and even unrelated product categories is an ongoing problem for ethical marketers. The decisions in cases brought to court have not always been consistent.

Some early cases of passing-off dealing with infringement of brand name were decided for the alleged infringer, and little or no protection was given to the original manufacturer despite the sale of identical goods under the same name (e.g., *Thomson v. Winchester*, 1837 and *Faber v. Faber*, 1867). However, some years later, in *Fischer v. Blank* (1893), courts recognized the importance of the total look of the object being sold. Despite different names, the total look of the package, or its Gestalt, was so similar that the infringer was found guilty by the courts and he could no longer sell his look-alike tea on the market.

Sometimes similar sounding names alone are used by competitors. The infringing name might only have to trigger an association or an image to the original to be found guilty of passing-off.

Taking well-established names to related or unrelated product categories is an important strategy that allows marketers to take advantage of their brand equity. However, when a brand name is taken to another product category by someone other than the original owner, some confusion as to the source of the product may exist on the part of the consumer. It is extremely important to protect one's brand name, even in non-competing markets.

Protection of far more than brand name is needed, as sometimes consumers do not identify only with the name, but use some other feature. The feature may or may not be associated with the name. For example, the Stiffel lamp was known by its shape and called by its name. The sea shell-shaped chocolates are identified by their shape and probably not by their brand name or manufacturer. It is the shape that is desirable.

Symbols may be attached to or associated with products. Tags on Levi's clothing identify their products as being produced by Levi. Similar tags on competitors' clothing caused some consumers to misidentify the clothes as manufactured by Levi.

Color in distinctive combinations or patterns can be critical to product or brand identification. There may be a problem in copyrighting certain colors, but when colors are coupled with other factors like shape or name, it may be easier to protect them. For example, if drugs of certain color combinations can also be linked to a certain shape, they may be more distinctly identified.

Imitating the trade dress or copying the Gestalt of a product or object is extremely common. Unscrupulous competitors seem to think that if they put their own brand name on a package or object that has been very successful in the marketplace, they will have no trouble selling their imitator brand. Fortunately, courts have generally upheld the rights of original manufacturers despite attempts by imitators to focus on minute differences that might exist.

Companies must also protect themselves from simple unpaid and unauthorized associations. Associations with positive images may contribute substantially to the infringers' profits. Associations with negative images may decrease the value of the original brand identity and lead consumers to avoid the original brand in the future. Thus future sales may be hurt by negative company images.

REFERENCES

Aaker, D. A. (1991). *Managing Brand Equity*. New York: The Free Press.

A & M Pet Products v. Pieces Inc. and Royal K-9, South West United States District Court, Central District of Los Angeles (1989).

Allison, J. R. (1978). Unfair competition. In T. W. Dunfee and J. D. Reitzel (eds.), *Business Law: Key Issues and Concepts*. Columbus, Ohio: Grid Publishing Inc.

American Cyanamid Co. v. United States Rubber Co., United States Court of Customers and Patent Appeals, 53 C.C.P.A. 994, 356 F.2d 1008 (1966).

American Greetings Corp. v. Dan-Dee Imports Inc., 619 F. Supp. 1204 (D.N.J.) (1985).

American Waltham Watch Co. v. United States Watch Co., Supreme Judicial Court of Massachusetts, 173 Mass. 85, 53 N.E. 141 (1899).

Bette Midler v. Ford Motor Co., 849 F2d 460 (9th Cir.) (1988).

Big O Tire Dealers v. Goodyear Tire and Rubber, United States Court of Appeals, Tenth Circuit, 561 F.2d 1365 (1977).

Chemical Corp. of America v. Anheuser-Busch Inc., 306 F.2d 433 (5th Cir. 1962), cert. denied, 372 U.S. 965 (1963).

Church & Dwight Co. Inc. v. Helene Curtis Industries Inc., Achter's Key Drug Inc., and N. W. A. Industries Inc., d.b.a. N. W. Ayer International, CCH. 61, 279 (D.C.N. Ill., January, 1977), BNA ATRR No. 802 (February 22, 1977), A-19.

Coach Leatherware Co. Inc. v. Ann Taylor Inc., 933 F2d 162, 18 USPQ2d 1907 (CA 2 1991).

Coca-Cola Co. v. Gemini Rising Inc., 346 F. Supp. 1183 (E.D.N.Y.) (1972).

Compco Corp. v. Day-Brite Lighting Inc., United States Supreme Court, 376 U.S. 234, 84 S. Ct. 779, 11 L. Ed. 2d 669 (1964).

Creem Magazine Inc. v. Modern Day Periodicals Inc., 76 Civ. 1804 (SDNY April 26) (1976).

Dallas Cowboys Cheerleaders Inc. v. Pussycat Cinema Ltd., 604 F. 2d 200 (2d Cir.) (1979).

Dallas Cowboys Cheerleaders Inc. v. Scoreboard Posters Inc., 600 F. 2d 1184 (5th Cir.) (1979).

Dell Publishing Company v. Norwood Publishing Company, 152 Misc. 213, 272 N.Y.S. 8 96 (Sup. Ct. N.Y. County) (1934).

Denicola, R. C. (1982). Trademarks as speech: Constitutional implications of the emerging rationales for the protection of trade symbols. *Wisconsin Law Review*, 158–207.

Dodds, W. B., Monroe, K. B., and Grewal, D. (1991). Effects of price, brand, and store information on buyers' product evaluations. *Journal of Marketing Research, Vol. 28* (August), 307–19.

Eastman Kodak Co. v. Fotomat Corp. (1969), 317 F. Supp. 304 N. D. Ga. 1969, appeal 441 F.2d 1079, 5th Cir., 1971.

Faber v. Faber, 49 Barb 3 Abb Pr (NS) 115 (NY Sup 1867), Cox 1892, supra note 5, cited in Pattishall, 1978, Vol. 68.

Felsenthal, E. (1992, July 16). Ice sculptors view this outcome as a means to a lasting legacy. *Wall Street Journal*, B1.

Fischer v. Blank, 138 N.Y. 244 N.E. 1040 (1893).

Fitzell, P. B. (1982). *Private Labels: Store Brands and Generic Products*. Westport, Conn.: Avi Publishing Co.

Fletcher, A. L. (1979). Buildings as trademarks. *Trademark Reporter, Vol. 69*, 229–45.

———. (1991). Trademark infringement and unfair competition in courts of general jurisdiction. *Trademark Reporter, Vol. 81*, 718–91.

Florence Mfg. Co. v. J. C. Dowd & Co., 178 F. 73, 75 (2d Cir.) (1910).

Fotomat Corp. v. Houck, 166 U.S.P.Q. 271 Fla. Cir. Ct., Pinellas County (1970).

General Electric Co. v. Alumpa Coal Co., 205 USPQ (BNA) 1036 (D. Mass. 1979).

Gibson, R. (1993, January 6). He hasn't got anything to spoof spaghetti and meat sauce—yet. *Wall Street Journal*, B1.

Girl Scouts of the United States v. Personality Posters Mfg. Co., 304 F. Supp. 1228 (S.D.N.Y.) (1969).

Goldman, K. (1992, February 14). American Express's ad snafu revives spot on creative pilfering. *Wall Street Journal*, B12.

Grotrian, Helfferich and Schulz v. Steinway & Sons, CA2 NY, 523 F2d 1331, 186 USPQ 436 (1975).

Grubbs, M. L. (1974). Trade protection for descriptive name and color. *Arkansas Law Review, Vol. 28*, 381–87.

Harold F. Ritchie Inc. v. Chesebrough-Ponds Inc., 281 F. 2d 755 (2d Cir.) (1960).

Hartford House Ltd., v. Hallmark Cards Inc., CA10 (Colo), 846 F2d 1268– Fed Cts 815, 862; Trade Reg 43, 334, 576, 626 (1986).

Hwang, S. L. (1992, October 23). It does sound like some B movie: Men from Mars vs. the green ones. *Wall Street Journal*, B1.

Inwood Laboratories Inc. v. Ives Laboratories Inc., U.S. 102 S. Ct. 2182, 72 L.Ed. 2d 606 (1982).

J. R. Wood & Sons Inc. v. Reese Jewelry Corp., 278 F. 2d 157 (2d Cir.) (1960).

John B. Stetson Co. v. Stephen L. Stetson Co. Ltd., 14 F. Supp. 74 (S.D.N.Y. 1936), modified and affirmed 85 F.2d 586 (2d Cir.) (1942). Cert. denied 299 U.S. 605, 57 S. Ct. 230, 81 L. Ed. 445; 128 F.2d 981.

John Walker & Sons Ltd. v. Modern Shoe Co., 213 F. 2d 322 (C.C.P.A.) (1954).

Keller, K. L. and Aaker, D. A. (1992). The effects of sequential introductions of brand extensions. *Journal of Marketing Research, Vol. 29* (February), 35–50.

LaTouraine Coffee Co. v. Lorraine Coffee Co., United States Court of Appeals, Second Circuit, 157 F. 2d 115 (1946).

Lego Australia Pty. Ltd. v. Paul's (Merchants) Pty. Ltd., Fed. Ct. of Australia. Gen. Divn., Sydney, July (1982).

Lego System A/S v. Lego M. Lemelstrich, 1983 F.S.R. 155 (Ch. D.).

LeSportsac v. K Mart Corp., CANY, 754 F2d 71.-Fed Cts 666; Trade Reg 11, 45, 349, 620, 621, 626, 629, 870 (1985).

Levi Strauss & Co. v. Blue Bell Inc., 632 F.2d 817 (9th Cir.) (1980).

Lucian Lelong Inc. v. George W. Button Corp., 50 F. Supp. 708 (S.D.N.Y.) (1943).

Maidenform Inc. v. Bestform Foundations Inc., Patent Office Trademark Trial and Appeal Board, 161 USPQ 805 (1969).

Maidenform Inc. v. Munsingwear Inc., United States District Court, Southern District, N.Y., 195 U.S.P.Q. 297 (1977).

Maternally Yours Inc. v. Your Maternity Shop Inc., 234 F. 2d 538, 546, 110 USPQ 462 (CA Z 1956).

McKelvey, S. (1993). NHL v. Pepsi-Cola Canada, uh-huh! Legal parameters of sports ambush marketing. *Entertainment and Sports Lawyer*, 5–17.

McWilliam's Wines Pty. Ltd. v. McDonald's System of Australia Pty. Ltd., Fed. Ct. of Australia. Gen. Divn (1980).

Merriam-Webster wins doubled award in Random House suit. (1991, November 22). *Publishers Weekly*, p. 13.

Motschenbacher v. R. J. Reynolds Tobacco Co., 498 F2d 821 (9th Cir.) (1974).

Narhex Australia Pty. Ltd. v. Sunspot Products Pty. Ltd., Federal Court of Australia, Perth (July, 1990).

National Hockey League v. Pepsi-Cola Canada Ltd./Pepsi-Cola Canada Ltee., Supreme Court of British Columbia, No. C902104 (June 2, 1992).

Norwich Pharmacal Co. v. Sterling Drug Inc. (1960), 271 F2d 569 (2d Cir. 1959), cert. denied, 362 U.S. 919.

Oppenheim, S. C. and Weston, G. E. (1977). *Unfair Trade Practices and Consumer Protection: Cases and Comments*. St. Paul, Minn.: West Publishing Co.

Oppenheim, S. C., Weston, G. E., Maggs, P. B., and Schechter, R. E. (1983). *Unfair Trade Practices and Consumer Protection: Cases and Comments*. St. Paul, Minn.: West Publishing Co.

Owens-Corning Fiberglass Corp., 774 F.2d 1116 (Fed Cir 1985).

Palace Station Inc. v. Ramada Station Inc., United States District Court, District of Nevada (1988).

Parkdale Custom Built Furniture Pty. Ltd. v. Puxu Pty. Ltd., High Court of Australia (1981–1982).

Pattishall, B. W. (1978). Two hundred years of American trademark law. *Trademark Reporter, Vol. 68* (March-April), 121–47.

Pillsbury Co. v. Milky Way Prods. Inc., 566 Pat. Trademark and Copyright J. (BNA) A-3 N.D. Ga. (Dec. 24, 1981).

Popular Merchandise Co. v. '21' Club Inc., United States Court of Customs and Patent Appeals, 52 C.C.P.A. 1224, 343 F. 2d 1011 (1965).

Price Pfister v. Mundo Corp.; Renco Sales Inc.; Laloo Manufacturing; Callahan Wholesale Hardware Co.; CWH Co.; Pioneer Industries Inc.; and Does 7 through 500 (1989), Superior Court of the State of California.

Safeway Stores Inc. v. Stephens, U.S. District Court for the Western District of Louisiana, 281 F. Supp. 517 (1967).

Schultz, A. B. (1977). Trade dress and unfair competition in publishing and packaging: When imitation is not the sincerest form of flattery. *Brooklyn Law Review, Vol. 43*, 643–79.

SCM Corp. v. Langis Foods Limited, United States Court of Appeals, District of Columbia, 539 F. 2d 196 (1976).

Sears, Roebuck & Co. v. Allstate Driving School Inc. (1969, ED NY), 301 F. Supp. 4, 163 USPQ 335.

Sears, Roebuck & Co. v. Stiffel Co., 376 U.S. 225, 84 S. Ct. 784, 11 L.Ed.2d 661 (1964).

Southwestern Bell Telephone Co. v. Nationwide Directory Service Inc., 371 F. Supp. 900 (W.D. Ark. 1974).

Stern, L. W. and Eovaldi, T. L. (1984). *Legal Aspects of Marketing Strategy: Antitrust and Consumer Protection Issues*. Englewood Cliffs, N.J.: Prentice-Hall Inc.

Sturm, Ruger & Co. Inc. v. Arcadia Machine & Tool Inc., United States District Court, Central District of California, (1988).

Swift & Co., 42 CCPA 1048, 223 F. 2d 950 (1955).

Taco Bell Pty. Ltd. v. Taco Company of Australia Inc., Fed. Ct. of Australia., Sydney (1981).

Thomson v. Winchester, 36 Mass (19 Pick) 214 (Sup. Ct.) (1837).

Tiffany & Co. v. Boston Club Inc., 231 F. Supp. 836 (d. Mass.) (1964).

Trademark protection of objects and configurations: A critical analysis. (1975). *Minnesota Law Review, Vol. 59*, 541–73.

Union Carbide Corp. v. Ever-Ready Inc., 531 F. 2d 366, 381–382, 188 USPQ
          623 (CA-7) (1976).

University of Notre Dame Du Lac v. Twentieth Century-Fox Film Corp., 22
          A.D.2d 452, 256 N.Y.S.2d 301, aff'd, 15 N.Y. 2d 940, 259 N.Y.S.2d
          832, 207 N.E.2d 508 (1965).

Vidal Sassoon Inc. v. Beverly Sassoon and Slim Lines Inc., United States
          District Court, Central Division of California (1982).

White, G. (1992, March 16). Japanese court hands Dodgers a sweet vic-
          tory. *Los Angeles Times*, p.D3.

Woo, J. (1992, September 30). He proved he knew his onions and pepper-
          oni, and sausage, etc. *Wall Street Journal*, B1.

World Carpets Inc. v. Dick Littrell's New World Carpets, United States Court
          of Appeals, Fifth Circuit, 438 F2d 482 (1971).

5

On Being Distinctive to Avoid Confusion

In order for the consumer to identify brands with their respective manufacturers, the brands must be sold with distinctive features supplied by that manufacturer. The distinctive features of one brand must be different from the features of a competitor's brand. This differentiation may be achieved through a well-known brand name, color, shape, particular look and feel, as well as the distinctive design of the package or product. Brand differentiation does not come without initial cost to the manufacturer. But after the initial costs, the manufacturer is entitled to reap certain benefits. Brand imitators want to enjoy the benefits without the associated costs.

The costs of differentiation are in the initial and additional dollars spent on production and marketing for differentiation, which may not be related to the quality or benefits of the product. For example, Owens-Corning manufactures Fiberglass Pink insulation, which is dyed pink. The pink color is an added cost with no value-added quality or necessary benefit to the product other than as identification. Between 1972 and 1981, Owens-Corning spent $42,421,000 on advertising to build a unique brand identification by associating its pink insulation with pink flamingos and the Pink

Panther cartoon character. This resulted in a 50 percent consumer association of pink insulation with Owens-Corning (Armstrong 1992: 604). Entry into the market is more expensive because of higher initial advertising costs while the consumer learns to identify the brand by its distinctive features. Other companies producing pink insulation had no reason to do so, other than that the public now associated quality insulation with pink insulation.

The benefits of a differentiation strategy, along with an extensive advertising campaign of the brand differentiation, should permit a company like Owens-Corning to acquire a control over price which it could not otherwise have achieved or maintained. The suggestion is that if manufacturers can differentiate their product in appearance and protect the distinction, purchasers will buy the product even though its quality is no greater than that of a non-differentiated product. Another benefit of product differentiation is that because of the advertising, purchase decisions are based partly on the advertising rather than on any active between-brand comparison of product attributes. The advertising should drive the purchase decision with little active thought given to the relative quality or source of the goods.

Brand imitators want to reap the benefits without any of the associated costs in developing distinctiveness. Being distinctive is not difficult, but it may be expensive.

BRAND NAMES

Because consumers rely heavily on brand names to identify goods and services for purchase, it is no wonder that unscrupulous competitors want to select a similar sounding brand name. Ethical competitors will select a name that is distinctly theirs when they want to stand behind their products on the marketplace. The kind of name selected for identifying one's goods might range from: 1) strong, distinctive, coined letter combinations that have no meaning, such as Xerox for photocopying; 2) less strong, inherently distinctive words that have a meaning in English but no reference or relationship to the goods or services associated with the mark, such as Crest for toothpaste; 3) relatively weak, inherently distinctive words that are suggestive rather than descriptive of the character or quality of the goods or services, such as Sunkist for oranges;

and 4) weak, inherently distinctive words that describe in a vague way the character or quality of the goods or services associated with the mark, such as Gardenfresh for frozen vegetables (Oyen 1982). Whatever the type of brand name desired by the company, the selection of the name should be a very careful process. The objective is to have the brand name distinctly linked only to the goods of the owner of the name. This is accomplished over time through extensive advertising with quality products, service, and image building.

How to Select a New Brand Name

The selection of a name for a new brand entering the market-place can be a long, costly, and tedious process requiring the services of a professional marketing research firm that specializes in the task. However, it can also be done by in-house brainstorming. An excellent five-point procedure for determining new names was outlined by McMurry (1954) in selection of the name Superlube, a new brand of lubricating oil. These five points may be applied to any new brand of product:

1. Interview purchasers as to what needs the product is expected to satisfy:
   a) preferences among existing brands
   b) reasons for preferences
   c) product expectations
   d) qualities the product should possess
2. Interview purchasers about existing brands:
   a) what names are known (have good attention and recall value)
   b) what names are preferred and why
   c) what these names suggest to the purchasers
3. Generate names for testing from:
   a) contests among employees and the public
   b) company's advertising agency
   c) an analysis of existing names
4. Have the names generated checked by the company's legal, advertising, and marketing departments to:
   a) eliminate those already in use or covered by copyrights
   b) eliminate those too similar to existing trade names
   c) eliminate those already in use with unrelated products

d) eliminate those that are obviously inappropriate (too long, too difficult to spell, or with unsuitable connotations)

5. Test the remaining brand names with a new sample of customers to determine:
   a) the extent to which the name suggested or implied it would satisfy the user's needs
   b) the extent to which the name could be easily remembered
   c) the extent to which the name suggests a quality product
   d) the extent to which associations clustering about the name were acceptable and would rouse a desire to purchase the brand

In following this procedure, 200 names were originally generated for the oil and the list was subsequently reduced to ten for final consumer testing (Bowen 1961). Superlube emerged as the best name for the company's product.

Case Study of Name Selection: Exxon. The amount of time, research, effort, and money that goes into the selection of a good brand name is demonstrated in the classic case of Standard Oil, New Jersey (Enis 1978). Standard Oil had four other company names at this time (Esso, Enco, Enjay, and Humble) and sought only one name to build its identity. Five names were also very expensive to keep up due to regional advertising, duplicate inventories of products and equipment, and continuing legal struggles to protect all the different brand names. More important, one of the world's largest corporations was seen by most of its customers as a regional company due to the five different names.

The company's objectives were to select a brand name that was easily identified on a worldwide basis, available and appropriate for use on a wide range of products, would convey a desirable image for all audiences, and would be free from legal restrictions on usage. Consumer analysis and research suggested that the new name should have no meaning at all and be very simple. The search for a new name began with a team of linguistic experts, a leading graphics-design firm, a battery of lawyers, and a computer. The computer search generated 10,000 words of four and five letters. More consumer research and testing reduced the number of names to 234. The name committee then cut that list to sixteen for further testing. Six names, including two existing trademarks (Enco and Enjay), were selected for final testing.

The six names were tested worldwide in 56 languages that are spoken by more than five million people. As a result, the two existing company names were eliminated: Enco, which meant 'stalled car' in Japanese, and Enjay, which had translation problems in Chinese. Exxon became the clear choice for both company and brand name. The research indicated that it conveyed the idea of a large, international enterprise, and portrayed the petroleum and chemical business in a way that was significantly superior to others. Exxon is easy to pronounce and remember, and it has no meaning in any language.

The next step was the development of the logo incorporating the brand name. Hundreds of combinations of shapes, colors, and designs were considered. The research procedures and techniques used included:

1. visibility tests using a tachistoscope to see how quickly and easily names and signs registered in conscious perception
2. memory tests in which the target emblems were presented in a matrix of other emblems
3. various tests of learning rates of different emblems
4. positive and negative association tests
5. design billboards to seen under various lighting conditions, from automobiles moving at 40 miles per hour (Enis 1978: 9).

After developing the name and logo, Exxon spent $100 million to promote its new identity. After just one month of advertising incorporating the new name, 92 percent of its company's customers and 88 percent of its competitors' customers were aware of the name change. Furthermore, one-half of those surveyed could cite why the name was changed. While the total amount spent on this process may seem outrageous, it should be viewed in relation to sales and profits. In 1973 alone, Exxon earned $2.4 billion on sales of $25.7 billion (Enis 1978). Therefore the cost of the name change might be viewed strictly as an investment.

The strength and distinctiveness of the Exxon trademark were subsequently tested in court (*Exxon Corp. v. Texas Motor Exchange of Houston Inc.*, 1980). The court decision was that the Exxon trademark was infringed by the mark "Texxon" but not by the mark "Tex-on." That one "x" made all the difference in consumer perception of identification and ownership. The court considered several points in its judgment. First, the Exxon mark was found to be a very strong, uncommon word, rarely used by others. Second, the design of the marks was not similar, even though both marks used block letters and similar colors. Third, the goods and services provided under each mark were similar (auto repairs). Fourth, the market for the goods was identical - members of the car-driving public. Fifth, the retail outlets were dissimilar, with Exxon using retail service stations and Texxon using warehouse type buildings. Sixth, the advertising media used by the parties were substantially identical; both used radio, television, newspaper, and yellow page advertising. Finally and perhaps most important, survey evidence indicated a high degree of confusion between the Texxon and Exxon marks, but no significant confusion when the Exxon and Tex-on marks were compared (Stern and Eovaldi 1984).

Protecting Brand Names

Once a brand name is selected by the company, it remains the exclusive property of its owner forever if it is not abandoned. The only other problem the manufacturer might encounter is if the trademark is lost through conversion to a generic term, as happened in *Anti-Monopoly Inc. v. General Mills Fun Group* (1979). In this case, Parker Bros. registered Monopoly as a trademark in 1935. In 1973, Anti-Monopoly was established to produce and sell a game it called Anti-Monopoly. Several consumer surveys were introduced as evidence, including one describing consumer motivation to purchase the product. The argument was that Monopoly had become a generic name. After several appeals, the court ruled that the survey evidence was erroneous and that Monopoly had become a word pertaining to the product rather than a brand of board game.

History shows that the manufacturers' own advertising or labeling is frequently at fault in these cases (Diamond 1982). Manufacturers generally strive to make their brand names household words. If a company is first in the market, it can reap profits by having a product so well-known that all other similar products become known by its name. Manufacturers often view this as an ideal situation. Consumers end up buying the trademark product because they are unsure whether competing products are of the same quality. The cost of this success is that other new brands may use the original brand name as their product name.

A trademark owner can take steps to prevent this. First, it can use the trademark as a descriptive adjective. A trademark identifies a particular brand of some product; hence grammatically it is an adjective. It is not the name of the product itself and it is not a noun. Because a trademark is an adjective, there must be a noun for it to modify. That noun is the generic name of the product. For example, Scotch Brand Tape, Sanka Brand Decaffeinated Coffee, or Vaseline Petroleum Jelly are uses of the generic product with the brand name (Diamond 1982).

Second, the manufacturer can make sure the media use the trademark properly to ensure that the consumer recognizes a trademark as a trademark. It can use the trademark notice in advertising and labeling.

Third, companies may display the mark with some form of special typographical treatment. Nothing contributes more strongly to the impression that a trademark is generic than its appearance in lowercase letters.

Fourth, if the trademark gets into the dictionary, the manufacturer can make sure it is identified as such. It can also extend the trademark name to other products, as Kimberly-Clarke Corp. has done with its Kleenex trademark. This informs consumers that the name represents a whole line of products (Verespej 1980).

All manufacturers want to avoid the situation in which the consumer starts asking his or her friends, "What brand of _____ do you use?" The blank space is filled, not with a generic such as the word coffee, but with a trademark, such as Sanka.

Case Study: Rollerblade. This company, with a recent innovation to the market constantly tries to remind consumers that its name is that of a company, not the product Rollerblade. Rollerblade Inc. sells a form of ice skates for pavement. Instead of a blade down the center, the bottom of the boot is a set of in-line wheels. Since this company was the innovator of the product category, it is constantly at risk of the public referring to the activity of using in-line skates as "roller-blading." Rollerblade Inc. must act very aggressively against any generic use of its trademark by other manufacturers or companies. If anyone uses "Rollerblade" in print as a general term or as a verb for in-line skating, the company sends a letter outlining correct usage. If an in-line skate manufacturer uses the name "Rollerblade" in any form with its product, it receives several warning letters and faces possible legal action (Goerne 1992).

Rollerbade also made itself more recognizable by selling a line of sportswear incorporating its brand name, "Blade Gear." By using the name "Blade" in the clothing line, it made the brand name more identifiable as a brand, rather than as a product. Rollerblade also differentiated its line by the use of neon colors, bright shoelaces, and high-tech boots. It relied on more than just the brand name to ensure that consumers identify "Rollerblade." Mainstream competitors of "Rollerblade" are also being ethical in their marketing practices by trying to differentiate their own brand name. The two main competitors are Bauer Precision In-Line Skates and First Team Sports' Ultra-Wheels.

The Bauer name is well known for ice skates. The company therefore wants customers to associate Bauer with in-line skates. It wants to capitalize on its own brand equity built up through its ice skates. Ultra-Wheels is committed to getting its own name more recognizable and to differentiating itself from "Rollerblade." It relies on celebrity endorsements from the National Hockey League player Wayne Gretzky to give its product credibility. The company also uses his actress wife, Janet Jones, to endorse the product to appeal to non-hockey fans. Both of "Rollerblade"'s main competitors are actively trying to differentiate and establish their own brand names in the marketplace.

In summary, Rollerblade is actively pursuing any misuse of its brand name; differentiating its product on more than brand name; and extending its brand name to other related product categories. Its competitors are heavily advertising their unique brand names in the marketplace. Successfully protecting one's brand name involves much more than attention to the brand name.

GESTALT

The marketplace should welcome competition. It is important to have different manufacturers producing the same products in order to reduce the prices paid by the consumer. However, the first manufacturer wants the competition to sell the goods in a different manner in order to differentiate them from its own. A good example of fair play in the marketplace based on total product presentation is demonstrated in the lawsuit of the *Kellogg Co. v. National Biscuit Co.* (1938) involving shredded wheat. Up until 1912 the National Biscuit Company held the patent on producing shredded wheat in biscuit pillow-shaped form. In that year the patent expired, and Kellogg started to produce shredded wheat. Kellogg took great effort to sell its product differently from its competitor and to associate its own brand name with its new product.

This differentiation was done in several ways. First, the standard Kellogg carton contained fifteen biscuits, while National Biscuit's contained twelve. The Kellogg cartons were distinctive in form and color, and the Kellogg label was distinct, bearing in bold script the names "Kellogg Whole Wheat Biscuit" or "Kellogg Shredded Whole Wheat Biscuit." It was perhaps impossible not to register the brand as a Kellogg product due to the size and spacing of the name.

The Kellogg biscuit was significantly smaller than that of National Biscuit, about two-thirds as large. It also had a different appearance. Therefore, consumers could easily tell the difference between the two brands even without the package. In this case, Kellogg took every reasonable precaution to prevent confusion or the practice of deception. The stimulus factors of size, color, and contrast were used to establish Kellogg's own brand identity, both on the package and with the product.

COLOR

It is very easy to use color to differentiate one's brand from a competitor's. The National Bureau of Standards is said to list 267 distinctive colors (Woo 1993). Given this vast array of colors to choose from, companies should have little difficulty selecting distinctive color combinations to identify themselves or their brands.

Although single colors are used in the marketplace, their protection may not be as straightforward as the use of distinctive combinations. A company cannot lay claim to a single hue unless there is overwhelming evidence that the customer identifies only that one brand or company with that particular color. This was the case in Owens-Corning Fiberglass and its pink fiberglass insulation and in *Master Distributors Inc. v. Pakor Inc.* and the sale of aquamarine splicing tape (Woo 1993). What is common in these cases is that the customers had asked for the product by color. The color was not an integral part of the product for function, but used as a cue for identification. These products could initially have been produced using another color, and there is no reason to believe that the success of the original product would have been any different.

While these companies were successful in building identification with one color as an integral quality cue for the product, the package or logo of the product is a more likely cue. Here, distinctive combinations and a particular design are crucial. If the company selects only a single hue for the package, there is a greater likelihood that a similar or even the same hue will be used by subsequent competing brands brought to the marketplace. For example, there are many brands of cola on the market with the same solid red color label as that used by Coca-Cola. There are fewer, if any, colas labeled or packaged in the blue, white, and red combinations of its rival Pepsi Cola. The more colors used in combination, the more difficult it may be to copy without blatantly infringing on the original. Therefore, when designing packages for new brands it is wise to use distinctive combinations of perhaps two or three colors to prevent imitation.

Sometimes, the defense in using the same color is that the color has somehow become generic for the product category. While some products do seem to have the same color, this is more convention than identification. Just as color can be an overriding cue for identification, it can also be used to help differentiate products. Products in the headache remedy category are overwhelmingly white. Nuprin used color to help set the pain reliever apart from its competitors (Santelmann 1988). Aspirins are always white, Tylenol is white, and Nuprin is yellow. Advertising the fact that Nuprin is yellow enhances the notion that Nuprin is different and creates a unique identity for the brand.

Color, whether in packaging or product make-up, is an easy cue to use to differentiate brands. Combinations of colors are superior to a single color for identification, because the protectability of a single color is extremely difficult and courts vary widely in their interpetation of the law on the issue of color as a trademark (Woo 1994).

SHAPE

Packages

Avoiding confusion by shape can be unrealistic in some markets and integral in others. Examples where shape is standard and difficult to differentiate are cereal boxes, cracker boxes, pasta boxes, and so on. Cardboard boxes are important packaging for some products, and the square shape makes the package very easy to display and stock. In these cases the design and color are even more critical to distinctive identity than the shape of the package.

Goods that are packaged in plastic or glass, on the other hand, are extremely easy to differentiate by shape. Shampoo bottles, perfume bottles, and deodorant bottles are but a few product categories where distinctively designed shapes lead to distinctive brand identity. Manufacturers of perfume put great effort into linking the distinctive shape of the perfume bottle to the brand name. This has been a relatively successful and ethical practice over the years.

The success is perhaps due to the fact that perfume is a relatively expensive product that conveys a strong image and meaning to the consumer. This is in contrast to a product like shampoo. Shampoo brands may develop distinctively shaped bottles, but their bottles are readily copied by competitors. Head and Shoulders is a brand that constantly suffers from imitation of the shape of the bottle.

When a distinctive shape is developed to identify the brand, it is important for the producer to emphasize the shape in its advertising. By doing this, the consumer will be more cognizant of the shape than the brand name. Due to the difficulty in obtaining a patent for shapes, it is important to build the product's shape in to its brand identity to create the secondary meaning. The protectability of package, container, and product configurations is outlined in Spratling (1973). However, these laws are under review, as evidenced by the discussions of the European Common Market (see Appendix). The more unique and fanciful the design, the more likely it is protectable.

The importance of shape to secondary meaning is exemplified in simple products such as chocolates. The distinctive shell-shaped chocolates produced by Chocolates a la Carte was held protectable by a court decision (Felsenthal 1992). Therefore, marketers should not underestimate the importance of shape in identification.

USE OF DISCLAIMERS

When copy artists try to avoid passing-off litigation, they some-times affix a statement that denies any connection to the original good. This is called a disclaimer. Disclaimers may be viewed in two ways. First, any company that thinks it needs to use a disclaimer is freely admitting that it has infringed on a trademark. Otherwise, why would it want to emphasize that there was no association? Just the presence of a disclaimer might be thought to imply a guilty party. The second view is that disclaimers are effective in alerting consumers who might mistakenly infer association. The legal rul-ings on this issue are far from conclusive and seem to vacillate between these two views of disclaimers (Palladino 1992). However, from the perspective of consumer behavior, there are clearly better and worse ways of setting up disclaimers. In other words, all disclaimers are not equal.

Attention and Disclaimers

The effectiveness or ineffectiveness of disclaimers might be ex-plained by the integration of attention and Weber's Law to the concept of advertising. When an advertisement contains many messages or words, figures, and pictures, attempts to emphasize any one message are more difficult. To focus attention on the main point in print ads, the advertiser can increase the size of the par-ticular printed message relative to the rest of the copy; supply it with a unique position or appearance; and/or repeat it several times.

When one wants some aspect of the message to be perceived, that aspect must be viewed relative to the complete presentation. A disclaimer may appear to attract attention when viewed in isolation. However, taken in context, this may not be so. One case that points out the importance of gaining attention is *Coca-Cola Co. v. Dorris* (1970).

In *Coca-Cola v. Dorris* (Erickson, Dunfee, and Gibson 1977) cus-tomers asked for Coke and received Dorris's cola. Coke was written on their receipt. The defendant had signs posted in Dorris House #1 that read: "We do not serve Coke or Coca-Cola. We serve Dorris House Cola." The courts ruled that the signs placed in the defendant's place of business were insufficient to constitute notice of the substitution of another product. The law does not place a burden on the customer to look for signs to ascertain what products are sold or are not sold in the retail outlet. The court stated that the customer must be verbally advised that the specified product is not available. In this case, the customer's attention was not directed to the sign. Given the total Gestalt of the restaurant, there is no reason for the customer to perceive the sign. The verbal notification would have provided context and contrast for the perception of the disclaimer.

Even if the disclaimer is brought to the attention of the consumer, the prior image and experience of the consumer may be too strong to give the disclaimer any weight. This was the case with *Elliot Knitwear Inc.* (1961). Elliot sold a sweater made of "Cashmora," which consumers thought meant cashmere. The Federal Trade Commission found that consumers would have the impression that it was cashmere even though the labels contained a statement of fiber and a disclaimer of cashmere content. The label "Cashmora" was accompanied by "No Cashmere" in smaller print below. After reading the label, 22 percent of viewers surveyed thought it contained cashmere. In this case the size of the disclaimer was probably overridden by the prior image and association of the words "cashmere" and "Cashmora."

The court articulated this phenomenon in a case involving the name of a restaurant (*Calamari Fisheries Inc. v. Village Catch Inc.* 1988). It concluded

that the use of the disclaimer could . . . become a subtle, indirect, and ironic means for the defendants to communicate and reinforce association with the plaintiff. Any disclaimer will appear to some customers to be little more than an attempt to impose a meaningless, hypertechnical legal requirement. By coupling the plaintiff's name with the defendant's establishment through litotic presentation of the plaintiff's protected name in a disclaimer, defendants will continue to achieve indirectly what they are proscribed even from suggesting directly. (Fletcher 1989: 850)

Effective Disclaimers

Previous examples have shown that disclaimers are usually ineffective to due to Weber's Law relating to the size and positioning of the disclaimer. There is a case of a disclaimer that is effective due to its size, color, and positioning, which all lead to good contrast effects. In *CBS Inc. v. Gusto Records Inc.* (1974), two record companies produced recordings of Charlie Rich. These records had different contents but were virtually the same product with the same name. The Gusto label contained old monograph songs and CBS wanted to stop the sale and distribution of Gusto in case customers confused the inferior recording with that of the CBS stereo album.

The court ordered a disclaimer be affixed directly over Charlie Rich's photograph. The position of the disclaimer was central to directing attention to it. The disclaimer was three and one-half inches by one and one-half inches large. It was therefore large enough to meet Weber's Law of threshold effects and to be perceived in the context of the record album, which is roughly a foot square. Finally, the decal was bright orange with black ink lettering. The color of the decal grabbed the attention of the customer, especially in contrast to the album background. These perceptual factors of size, color, positioning, and contrast likely led to a successful disclaimer that was perceived by the customer. The same disclaimer in a dark color an a smaller label, put on the back of the album, would likely not have been perceived by the consumer.

Ineffective Disclaimers

Unfortunately, most disclaimers follow the example of *John B. Stetson Co. v. Stephen L. Stetson Co. Ltd.* (1942). In this case, the courts stipulated that a disclaimer be put on the defendant's hats and use in its advertising. The decree provided that in any advertising done by the defendant, the dividing words "Never Connected In Any Way" should be printed in letters substantially larger and in bolder type than any printing above or below it. An exception was made for the linings and labels inside of caps or hats. The disclaimer could be printed curved upward immediately adjacent to the other part of the label and in letters of the same size and boldness of the other words.

While the court had good intentions, the defendant was adept at rendering the disclaimer totally ineffective. Over time, the disclaimer became part of the background design of the label in the hats and was virtually lost in any advertising. The look of the disclaimer on the hats was: the name "Stephen L. Stetson" in headline type on the entire first line; the corporate name and address in large type on the bottom lines; the disclaimer surrounded by ornamental scroll; and the words "Never Connected" printed in letters one-sixth the size of the name. In the display ads, the name "Stephen L. Stetson" appeared in huge type five times and once in the corporate name, while the disclaimer was tucked away in an obscure margin or corner.

Several perceptual factors accounted for the ineffectiveness of the disclaimer: figure and ground, size, context, and primacy or recency. The disclaimer was the background, not the figure or center of attention. In fact, it looked like a decoration. The disclaimer was so much smaller than the rest of the print that it was probably below the perception threshold level of the consumer. It was also buried in the middle of the text, rendering neither a primacy or recency effect.

Summary. Even if disclaimers are the center of attention, the association may be so complete in the mind of the consumer that very little can be done to distinguish the original brand. In *Vidal Sassoon Inc. v. Beverly Sassoon and Slim Lines Inc.* (1982), Harold Kassarjian, the noted scholar of consumer behavior, stated in his declaration:

[B]ased on my knowledge of information processing and consumer perception of advertising and labels, my conclusion is that a written or oral disclaimer of association with Vidal Sassoon would not be an effective solution. Many potential customers would simply be oblivious to a disclaimer, or ignore it. Others would focus on or notice the words "Vidal Sassoon" and conclude that the product was produced by Sassoon. Still other consumers would misperceive a disclaimer as actually an endorsement of the product by Vidal Sassoon, Inc. and Beverly Sassoon. Finally a group of consumers might perceive a disclaimer as it is intended to be understood. Nevertheless, the risks of placing a disclaimer on the product are great. *There is greater* probability that the message will be ignored or misunderstood than there is that it will be perceived as intended. It is even possible that a majority of consumers would misperceive or ignore any disclaimer. (pp. 6–7)

Given the aging of the population and the increased need for reading glasses, it is likely that more and more consumers will not be able to read disclaimers, even if they are brought to their attention, when shopping in the marketplace.

How to Set up Disclaimers

Guidelines for disclaimers are put forth for industry by the Federal Trade Commission in the United States. These are not laws, but self-administered guidelines. There are many deficiences in the disclosure program due to the information-processing limitations of consumers (see Stoltman, Morgan, & Muehling 1991 for a complete discussion), but the first step is to implement the recommended procedure for disclosures or disclaimers.

Television Disclaimers. The Federal Trade Commission (1979) has an enforcement policy statement with regard to clear and conspicuous disclosures in television advertising. The words "clear and conspicuous" refer to the technical factors (size of letters, duration of disclosure, etc.) used in presenting the disclosure to a television audience, as well as to the substance of the individual disclosure. The commission believes that the following standards should be met for a television disclosure to be deemed clear and conspicuous.

1. The disclosure should be presented simultaneously in both the audio and video portions of the television advertisement.
2. The video portion of the disclosure must contain letters of sufficient size so that it can be easily seen and read on all television sets, regardless of picture tube size, that are commercially available to the public.
3. The video portion of the disclosure should contain letters of a color or shade that readily contrasts with the background. The background should consist of only one color of shade.
4. During the audio portion of the disclosure, no other sounds, including music, should be presented.
5. The video portion of the disclosure should appear on the screen for a sufficient duration to enable it to be completely read by the viewer.
6. The audio and video portions of the disclosure should immediately follow the specific sales representation to which it relates, and should be presented each time the representation is presented during the advertisement. In cases where a disclosure is required but is not linked to a specific representation, it should appear in immediate conjunction with the major sales theme of the advertisement (Federal Trade Commission 1979: 114–15).

Print Disclaimers. Getting similar messages across to consumers in print requires specific detailing of the size of the message in relation to the size of the package or advertisement. This is another application of Weber's Law and the relative size of the disclaimer in relation to its context. One example of print messages are health warnings that are now part of alcohol labeling in the United States (Code of Federal Regulations 1992). The guidelines are:

1. The warning must be stated on the brand label or separate front label or on a back or side label separate and apart from all other information.
2. The warning must be on a contrasting background.
3. The words "GOVERNMENT WARNING" must be in bold letters and capitals. The remainder of the warning must not appear in bold type.
4. The warning statement shall appear in a maximum number of characters per inch as follows:
    a) maximum of forty characters when type size is one millimeter.
    b) maximum of twenty-five characters when type size is two millimeters
    c) maximum of twelve characters when type size is three millimeters.
5. The size of type shall be proportional to the size of container:
    a) containers of eight ounces or less, a minimum of one millimeter
    b) containers between eight ounces and 101 ounces, a minimum of two millimeters
    c) containers larger than 101 ounces, a minimum of three millimeters.
6. The labels must be firmly affixed so that neither water or other solvents will remove them.

The Canadian Department of Consumer and Corporate Affairs has also outlined some very general rules about print disclaimers (Misleading Advertising Bulletin 1990). Canadian guidelines cover the content, placement, format, symbols used, symbol placement, and size of the fine print. They generally recognize the effects of size and placement of the disclaimer on the consumer's perception of the information. The usual placement of disclaimers in small print at the bottom of the message usually ensures the very opposite results of the reason for using a disclaimer in the first place. If the information in the disclosure is intended to be read and absorbed, it should be included in the main part of the message in a format likely to be read and understood, and not at the bottom of the message in fine print.

One of the reasons given for the use of disclaimers is that advertisers believe they can avoid charges of misleading advertising through them. This was the case in *National Hockey League v. Pepsi Cola Canada Ltd.* (1992). Pepsi was accused of using the National Hockey League in its soda pop promotion without the league's authorization. Pepsi included a disclaimer on its television advertising that was not perceived by 99 percent of those exposed to the advertisement during a mall-intercept marketing research study. Pepsi also included the disclaimer in fine print on the back of its contest entry form. Consumer research showed that 68 percent of those surveyed thought that the NHL was either sponsoring or associated with the Pepsi promotion. The judge read the disclaimer (with his reading glasses) and announced that anyone carefully reading the disclaimer could not possibly be confused as to any association or sponsorship. The problem was that the vast majority of consumers never read the disclaimer or had any idea there was a disclaimer present.

SUMMARY

Avoiding a competitor's imitation is not an easy task. Manufacturers must think seriously about the prevention of trademark infringement when developing their brands and products. Because only very successful brands, such as product category leaders, are copied, it may be difficult to remain aware of the possibility of infringement during development. It is rare to have a crystal ball that would tell of the future success of the brand. The major areas to be aware of in creating distinctive brands are:

1. Brand names in a product class should be unique in terms of sound, pronunciation, spelling, and meaning. A company should use the brand name preceding the name of the product category to reinforce the brand name to customers. For example, the manufacturer would refer to Breton crackers in advertising, not just Breton's.

2. Color combinations are superior to single colors for brand identification. The protection of color combinations in the courtroom is much easier than protection of a single color.

3. The Gestalt or total look of the brand, whether it be the product consumed or just the package, is important to distinctive identity. The combination of size, color, design or picture, brand name, and shape all give the consumer's eye the "look" of the brand. Distinctly different names of brands may not be enough to form distinctly different identities in the mind of the consumer. Consumers purchase from many product categories, not by brand name, but by the "look" of the product.

4. Unique shapes of containers, packages, or products help to create a distinctive identity. These unique shapes might be best coupled, where possible, with distinctive colored labels for identification.

The use of disclaimers by a company to provide distinction is misguided. If a company thinks it needs to use a disclaimer, it is likely to be infringing on another's trademark or trade dress. Brands should speak for themselves, not the fine print.

REFERENCES

Anti-Monopoly Inc. v. General Mills Fun Group, 611 F. 2d 296, 301 (9th Cir.) (1979).

Armstrong, J. S. (1992). Secondary meaning "in the making" in trademark infringement actions under Section 43 (9) of the Lanham Act. *George Mason University Law Review, 14* (Summer), No. 3, 603–35.

Consumer and Corporate Affairs (1990). *Asterisks, disclaimers, and other fine print* (Misleading Advertising Bulletin 4). Director of Investigation and Research, Competition Act, Canada.

Bowen, D. C. (1961). Applied psychology and trademarks. *The Trademark Reporter, Vol. 51,* 1–26.

Calamari Fisheries Inc. v. Village Catch Inc., 698 F. Supp. 994, 997, 8 USPQ2d 1953, 1954 (D. Mass 1988).

CBS Inc. v. Gusto Records Inc. U.S. District Court for the Middle District of Tennessee, 403 F. Supp. 447 (1974).

Coca-Cola Co. v. Dorris, 311 F. Supp. 287 (E. D. Ark.) (1970).

Diamond, S. A. (1982). Properly used, trademarks are forever. *American Bar Association* (December), 1575–79.

Elliot Knitwear Inc. 59 F.T.C. 893, 904, 911 (1961).

Enis, B. M. (1978). Exxon marks the spot. *Journal of Advertising Research* (December), 7–12.

Erickson, M. L., Dunfee, T. W., and Gibson, F. F. (1977). *Antitrust and Trade Regulation.* Columbus, Ohio.: Grid.

Exxon Corp. v. Texas Motor Exchange of Houston Inc., 628 F. 2d 500 (5th Cir.) (1980).

Federal Register National Archives and Records Administration. (1992). *Code of Federal Regulations: Alcohol, Tobacco Products, and Firearms, 27*, 204.

Federal Trade Commission (1979). Consumer information remedies policy session. *FTC Bureau of Consumer Protection* (June).

Felsenthal, E. (1992, July 16). Ice sculptors view this outcome as a means to a lasting legacy. *Wall Street Journal*, B1.

Fletcher, A. L. (1989). Trademark infringement and unfair competition in courts of general jurisdiction. *Trademark Reporter, Vol. 79*, 794–882.

Goerne, C. (1992, March 2). Rollerblade reminds everyone that its success is not generic. *Marketing News*, p.1.

John B. Stetson Co. v. Stephen L. Stetson Co. Ltd. 14 F. Supp. 74 (S.D.N.Y. 1936). Modified and affirmed 85 F.2d 586 (2d Cir.), cert. denied 299 U.S. 605, 57 S. Ct. 230, 81 L. Ed. 445: 128 F.2d 981 (1942).

Kellogg Co. v. National Biscuit Co., 305 U.S. 411, 422 (1938).

McMurry, R. N. (1954). How to pick a name for a new product. *Sales Management, Vol. 73*, 102.

National Hockey League v. Pepsi Cola Canada Ltd./Pepsi Cola Canada Ltd. Supreme Court of British Columbia, No. C902104 (1992, June 2).

Oyen, G. O. S. Clearly descriptive trademarks - Drawing the line in the wake of the OFF! decision. 13–65 C.P.R. (2d) (1982).

Palladino, V. N. (1992). Disclaimers before and after HBO v. Showtime. *Trademark Reporter, Vol. 82*, 203–22.

Santelmann, N. (1988, May 2). Color that yells, "buy me." *Forbes*, p. 110.

Spratling, G. R. (1973). The protectability of package, container, and product configurations. *Trademark Reporter, Vol. 63*, 117–52.

Stern, L. W. and Eovaldi, T. L. (1984). *Legal Aspects of Marketing Strategy: Antitrust and Consumer Protection Issues*. Englewood Cliffs, N.J.: Prentice-Hall.

Stoltman, J., Morgan, F., and Muehling, D. D. (1991). Televised advertising disclosures: A review and synthesis. In R. Holman (ed.), *Proceedings of the 1991 Conference of the American Academy of Advertising*. New York: American Academy of Advertising, p. 16.

Trademark protection of objects and configurations: A critical analysis. (1975). *Minnesota Law Review, Vol. 59*, 541–73.

Verespej, M. A. (1980, April 14). When is a trademark not a trademark? *Industry Week*, 69–73.

Vidal Sassoon Inc. v. Beverly Sassoon and Slim Lines Inc. United States District Court, Central District of California, No. 82–2916 WMP (1982).

Woo, J. (1993, February 25). Trademark law protects colors, court rules. *Wall Street Journal*, B1.

———. (1994, January 5). Product's color alone can't get trademark protection. *Wall Street Journal*, B5.

6

Testing for Brand Imitation

One thing to remember about any research study is that it will never be perfect. Even when the most experienced researchers work collectively without any time constraints or pressure, flaws appear only after the work is complete and the results are studied. Research is undertaken to discover, and in that process of discovery, under incomplete information, researchers learn where to take their next inquiry. Therefore, there is little chance that research done for litigation purposes, often by a sole researcher sworn to secrecy about the project, can produce perfect work under considerable time constraints. This should be understood by all parties involved before the research is undertaken.

Professional people will do the best job possible given their information and time limitations. Market research by highly trained professionals rarely has "fatal" flaws. It almost always has minor flaws that could be improved. Arguing over minor flaws is a favorite tactic of litigation lawyers, who try to divert attention from major issues and discredit the professionals who did the research. Minor flaws might also be used by judges to devalue the consumer research so that they may be more comfortable making a ruling based on their own personal opinion of the evidence before them.

A survey of field research submitted in Trademark Cases (Jacoby 1985) shows that in only fourteen out of sixty-seven instances was the research accorded substantial weight (see Exhibit 6.1). Why the consumer research did not play a major role in most of the cases was not always documented by the court. It seems that consumer data collected for cases of trademark infringement play a very uncertain role. Part of this uncertainty may be the result of blurring between public opinion poll research methodology and market research methodology.

Research in trademark infringement is based on marketing. Marketing research, at the consumer level, usually relies on consumers' reactions to the marketing stimuli. The aim of the research is to measure the consumers' perceptions and reactions to the product, service, or communication strategy, under very controlled conditions. The techniques and methods used to measure reactions are usually experimental in nature and carried out with relatively small samples. Test marketing for products is different from polling the public for election results or the sentiments of the population. Public opinion polls usually require random sampling of the population in some proportional representative manner so that predictions of public sentiment can be made. The criteria and methods for public opinion polling are different from the criteria and methods for consumer research for marketing purposes. The two different areas require different tools from the social scientist.

This point is important because the courts, legal scholars, and attorneys have erroneously labeled all field research as "surveys" or "public opinion polls" (Jacoby 1985: 197). In fact, the research done in trademark infringement cases rarely consists of surveys or public opinion polls. Data from relevant consumers are usually gathered to support or provide evidence of the relevant points in each case of trademark infringement. Some of the most common evidence may be in the form of primary data collected by the parties from consumers of their goods. The type of data and techniques used to generate the data will vary by the nature of the issue.

HOW LARGE A SAMPLE?

The first question usually asked in designing research is: How many people do I need to sample? It is an important question that

EXHIBIT 6.1
Field Research Submitted in Trademark Cases

Number	Parties (year)	Court[a]	Offeror[b]	Admitted	Weight
1	Sears Roebuck v. All States Insurance (1957)	A	P	no	-
2	American Luggage v. U.S. Trunk (1957)	D	P	yes	little
3	Jenkins Bros. v. Newman Hender & Co. (1961)	A	P	yes	"not persuasive"
4	American Thermos v. Aladdin Industries (1962)	D	P	yes	little
5	American Thermos v. Aladdin Industries (1962)	D	D	yes	substantial
6	Zippo Manufacturing v. Rogers Import (1963)	D	P	yes	substantial
7	GM Corp v. Cadillac Marine Corp. (1964)	D	P	yes	little to none
8	Donald F. Duncan Inc. v. Royal Tops (1965)	A	P	no	-
9	Humble Oil v. American Oil (1966)	D	P	yes	moderate
10	Humble Oil v. American Oil (1966)	D	D	yes	moderate
11	Sears Roebuck v. Allstate Driving School (1969)	D	P	yes	"little"
12	Burrough Ltd. v. Lesher d/b/a Beefeaters (1969)	D	D	yes	some
13	Am Basketball Assoc. v. AMF Voit Inc. (1973)	D	P	yes	not given "substantial weight"
14	LaMaur Inc. v. Alberto-Culver (1973)	D	P	yes	not "of significant assistance"
15	LaMaur Inc. v. Alberto-Culver (1973)	D	D	yes	not "of significant assistance"
16	Holiday Inns v. Holiday Out in America (1973)	A	P	yes	"little", "slight"
17	Grotrian-Steinweg v. Steinway & Sons (1973)	D	P1	yes	substantial
18	Grotrian-Steinweg v. Steinway & Sons (1973)	D	P2	yes	substantial
19	Union Carbide v. Ever-Ready (1975)	D	P1	yes	"little if any weight"
20	Union carbide v. Ever-Ready (1975)	D	P2	yes	"little if any weight"
21	Jockey International v. Burkhard (1975)	D	D	yes	little
22	National Football League v. Dallas Cap (1975)	A	P	yes	some
23	McNeil Laboratories v. Am. Home Products (1976)	D	D	yes	some
24	J. Burrough Ltd. v. Sign of the Beefeater (1976)	A	P	yes	substantial
25	Fremont v. ITT Continental Baking (1977)	D	D	yes	some
26	WGBH Ed. Foundation v. Penthouse (1978)	D	D	yes	little to none
27	Astatic Corp. v. American Electronics (1979)	D	P	yes	little to none
28	RJR Foods v. White Rock Corp. (1979)	A	P	yes	some
29	American Footwear v. General Footwear (1979)	A	D1	no	"rejected"
30	American Footwear v. General Footwear (1979)	A	D2	no	"rejected"
31	Amstar v. Domino's Pizza (1980)	A	P	yes	"substantially defective"
32	Amstar v. Domino's Pizza (1980)	A	D	yes	none
33	Exxon v. Texas Motor Exchange (1980)	A	P	yes	"great"
34	Loctite v. National Starch (1981)	D	D1	Yes	none
35	Loctite v. National Starch (1981)	D	D2	yes	none
36	Scotch Whiskey v. Consolidated Distillers (1981)	D	P	yes	"great", "particularly persuasive"
37	Anti-Monopoly v. General Mills (1981)	D	P	yes	none
38	Brooks Shoe v. Suave Shoe (1981)	D	P	yes	little
39	Brooks Shoe v. Suave Shoe (1981)	D	D	yes	considerable
40	National Football League v. Wichita Falls (1982)	D	P	yes	considerable
41	Tomy Corp. v. P.G. Continental (1982)	D	P	yes	irrelevant
42	Deere & Co. v. Farmhand (1982)	D	P	yes	none
43	Deere & Co. v. Farmhand (1982)	D	P2	yes	none
44	Anti-Monopoly v. General Mills Fun Group (1982)	A	D	yes	"no relevance"
45	Anti-Monopoly v. General Mills Fun Group (1982)	A	P1	yes	"compelling evidence"
46	Anti-Monopoly v. General Mills Fun Group (1982)	A	P2	yes	substantial
47	Levi Strauss v. Blue Bell (1982)	D	D	yes	considerable
48	Levi Strauss v. Blue Bell (1982)	D	P	yes	little
49	Prudential Ins. Co. v. Gibraltar Corp. (1982)	A	P	yes	none
50	U.S. International Trade Comm. v. Certain Cubes (1982)	A	P	yes	some
51	U.S. International Trade Comm. v. Certain Cubes (1982)	A	D	yes	none
52	Plus Products v. Plus Discount Foods (1983)	D	P	yes	"limited"
53	Toys "R" Us v. Canarsie Kiddie Shop (1983)	D	P	no	
54	Mennen v. Gillette (1983)	D	P	yes	none
55	Aris Isotoner v. Fownes Bros. (1983)	D	P	yes	little
56	Aris Isotoner v. Fownes Bros. (1983)	D	D	yes	little
57	Nestle v. Chester's Market (1983)	D	D1	yes	some
58	Nestle v. Chester's Market (1983)	D	D2	yes	some
59	Nestle v. Chester's Market (1983)	D	P1	no	-
60	Nestle v. Chester's Market (1983)	D	P2	yes	"no bearing"
61	Nestle v. Chester's Market (1983)	D	P3	yes	none
62	Nestle v. Chester's Market (1983)	D	P4	no	-
63	Henri's Food Products v. Kraft (1983)	A	D1	yes	none
64	Henri's Food Products v. Kraft (1983)	A	D2	yes	some
65	Brooks Shoe v. Suave Shoe (1983)	A	P	yes	little
66	Brooks Shoe v. Suave Shoe (1983)	A	D	yes	considerable

[a] D = U.S. District Court; A = U.S. Appeals Court
[b] D = Defendant; P = Plaintiff

Source: Jacoby, J. (1985). "Survey and Field Experimental Evidence" in *The Psychology of Evidence and Trial Procedure*, Saul M. Kassin and Lawrence S. Wrighsman (eds.) Beverly Hills: Sage Publications, pp. 188–89.

affects the cost of the research and the time taken to complete the data collection. The number of subjects needed for any survey or study depends on the question being asked, the critical effect size, and the statistical power desired by the researcher. A misunderstanding of statistical power or ability of the study to detect real differences often leads to waste in time, money, and effort in sampling too many or too few people to make the study meaningful. A misunderstanding of critical effect may lead to under-sampling if the critical effect is very small, and over-sampling if the critical effect is relatively large. (For a detailed explanation of these concepts, see Chumura Kraemer and Thiemann 1987.)

Critical Effect

The critical effect relates to the central question of how many subjects out of what size sample or what percent of the population need to be confused for the court to rule that confusion occurs beyond a reasonable doubt in the marketplace. A "substantial" or "appreciable" number of consumers need not be a majority of the total consumers. This distinction may be crucial where a study shows a low percentage of confused customers that can be extrapolated over a large relevant "universe" of potential customers. For example, in the case of *Humble Oil and Refining Co. v. American Oil Co.* (1969), the court indicated that 11 percent of a national market of millions of consumers constitutes a very large number of potential confused consumers. Another example might be the billion-dollar soft drink industry, where 1 percent of consumers might mean millions of dollars and people. In these cases, the critical effect may be very small and larger samples are therefore needed to find that important 1 percent.

In cases where the critical effect is predetermined to be very large—for example, if over 50 percent of consumers are perceived as necessary evidence to indicate likelihood of confusion—then smaller samples will suffice. The critical effect is also related to the degree of confidence researchers want to have in their statement about the likelihood of confusion among consumers.

The number or percentage of consumers who need to be confused with respect to the object of investigation is a matter that seems to vary widely in the courts. The courts may do some of the calculation intuitively, as figures of 8.5 percent (*Grotrian, Helfferich, Schultz Steinweg Nach v. Steinway and Sons* 1975); 11 percent (*Jockey International Inc. v. Burkard* 1975); or 15 percent to 20 percent (*RJR Foods Inc. v. White Rock Corp.* 1978) have all been found to indicate confusion among the consuming public.

A Canadian colleague conveyed an experience in which the judge ruled that if the plaintiff showed just one individual who was confused as to the origin of goods, that was enough to find confusion in the marketplace. Although this might seem odd, judges are in control of their courtrooms and one witness may represent a large number of other people (Bonynge 1962). Clearly, this example is extreme, but nonetheless there is wide variation in the levels of confusion required by judges. The overall average percentage of confusion judged by the courts to constitute a critical level is about 20 to 25 (Preston 1990). That means at least 20 percent to 25 percent of potential customers are likely to confuse, mistake, or associate the two objects in question.

The courts may also change their minds. In *Coca-Cola Co. v. Tropicana Prods. Inc.* (1982), a 15 percent level of confusion among consumers was initially determined not to support a finding of deceptiveness, but on appeal, the higher court ruled that less than 15 percent was sufficient to find deceptiveness in the marketplace (Preston 1990). The legal system is a matter of precedent, and levels of confusion found in past cases may be extrapolated to present and future court cases. Cases with high levels of confusion are held as well as those with low levels of confusion.

Another issue with respect to the required level of confusion is that there may be a double standard concerning harm to consumers and their costs, as compared with harm to corporations and their profits. In many cases involving frequently branded goods, where the consumer easily interchanges brands under low involvement, more harm due to consumer confusion or passing-off may be done to the company than to the consumer. That is, the original company suffers loss of sales, but the consumer is not perceived by the courts as being harmed. When the consumer suffers no threat of personal injury or incurs no apparent costs, the courts might require a higher level of confusion to be present in the marketplace.

When consumers suffer obvious harm or personal injury due to their confusion or perceptions of association, a smaller percentage might be judged to be the criterion. The courts may thus have a double standard with respect to protecting the consumer and protecting the large company. When it is evident that consumers are greatly harmed by inferior products, perhaps a smaller percentage will justify confusion. When the company is mainly harmed by lost sales and there seems to be little or no harm done to the customers, the courts may want a higher level of confusion to justify action. However, this is only speculation.

Significance level. To give some understanding of the relationships among critical effect, significance level (or the probability of results happening by chance), and sample size, the following situation is offered. Copycat trade dress is often thought of as infringing on an original or as being too similar to the original successful brand. Manufacturers do not usually go to court because they think a competitor's trade dress is *not* infringing or is different from the original. Therefore, most statistical testing in these cases involves what is called a one-tailed test in statistics. In other words, the interest is only in the fact the two items are similar, not that they are different. The statistical test to see if two items are similar or different would involve a two-tailed test, in that both outcomes are tested at the same time. The importance of distinguishing between testing for differences and similarities or just for similarities is that smaller samples are needed for one-tailed tests. This is because we do not need the "power" to test for differences, just the "power" to test for similarities.

The second point to make is with respect to significance level, or the probability that the outcome occurred by chance rather than confusion. The significance level is usually reported as $p < 0.01$, $p < 0.05$, or $p < 0.10$. $P < 0.01$ means that the odds are one in 100 that the finding occurred by chance. The usual significance level accepted in social science research is one in twenty, or $p < 0.05$. However, one in ten, or $p < 0.10$, may be adequate depending on the problem and sample size. Clearly, one in 100 or $p < 0.01$, leads to greater confidence in the outcome. It exhibits very strongly that the results are unlikely to have happened by chance. However, many researchers are comfortable using a $p < .05$ level in their interpretation of the results.

The researcher may select the confidence level in advance, depending on how confident he or she wants to be in the results. The appropriate confidence level also may relate to sample sizes. Large samples should use smaller probability levels. Smaller samples (perhaps under twenty) may find $p < 0.10$ quite acceptable. Underlying this discussion with regard to statistical inferences is the notion of normally distributed responses. Detailed discussion of this concept is beyond the scope of this book, but generally speaking, a larger sample (greater than thirty) will be more likely to have a normal distribution.

Number of Subjects

Given a one-tailed test and a $p < 0.05$ confidence level, the next step is to examine the critical effect or level of confusion that is deemed necessary to represent real confusion on the part of the consumer. Once the necessary critical-effect size is chosen, the number of subjects required to find that effect can be determined. An analysis of prior court cases gives some indication of the critical effect or necessary number of people who have to be confused in order to confirm the presence of infringement. Table 6.1 lists the level of confusion (or criterion level) found within the sample in various passing-off cases. Using the percentage of customers confused, Table 6.1 provides an estimate of the number of subjects needed to achieve the criterion using different probability levels and confidences in achieving that result. The 99 percent power level may be interpreted as close to certainty.

The research design needs more participants when the confusion of a small percentage of consumers is an important consideration. When a large percentage of the people need to be confused, a smaller sample will suffice. Gathering data from large samples, say 300, when the criterion is 50 percent confusion leads the researcher to be extremely confident that more than enough people have participated in the survey to find that level of confusion.

Just what the criterion for confusion should be varies with the problem. However, Preston (1990) notes that a likely criterion is 20 percent to 25 percent or more. Given that baseline, the sample sizes at different power levels are listed in Table 6.2.

Smaller sample sizes are therefore needed to find higher levels of confusion. To gather data to determine the preset level of confusion from samples that are larger than needed may be a waste of

Table 6.1
Prior Passing-off Cases: Projected Sample Sizes Needed Over Different Power Levels

CASE	Research Results % Confused in Case	Sample Size Needed to Achieve Power Level One-Tailed[1] Test at p<.01[2] (p<.05)[3]		
		99[4]% ~N[5]	90% ~N	80% ~N
Grotrian, et al. v. Steinway & Sons (1975)	8.5%	3000 (2200)	1800 (1200)	1400 (800)
Jockey International v. Burkard (1975)	11%	1776 (1294)	1069 (704)	824 (508)
RJR Foods v. White Rock (1978)	15-20%	949-528 (692-385)	571-318 (376-210)	441-246 (272-152)
NFL v. Delaware (1977)	19-20%	587-528 (428-385)	353-318 (233-210)	273-246 (169-152)
Smith v. Sturm, Ruger (1985)	39%	130 (110)	79 (63)	57 (48)
Federal Glass Co. v. Corning Glass Works (1969)	52%	70 (50)	45 (35)	35 (20)
International Milling v. Robin Hood Popcorn (1956)	61.5%	45 (32)	28 (18)	21 (14)
NHL v. Pepsi-Cola Canada (1992)	68%	34 (25)	19 (14)	15 (11)

[1]Only tests if the two are similar.
[2]One in a hundred this will occur by chance.
[3]One in twenty this will occur by chance.
[4]Power to find a significant result.
[5]Sample size.

money and effort. However, the determination of sample size is made from many factors, and the exact criterion level may not be known before data collection. Most researchers would be comfortable functioning at $p < 0.05$ and at a 90 percent power level. This would allow for a level of confusion of about 16 percent to 17 percent using a sample of 300 consumers. But in the soft drink sample, where 1 percent or 2 percent confusion could mean millions of dollars, a sample of 10,000 to 15,000 consumers might be needed to find that 1 percent of the confused consumers.

Table 6.2
Sample Sizes Required at Different Confusion Criteria and Power Levels

Confusion Criterion	Power at p<.05		
	95%	90%	80%
20%	265	210	152
30%	114	91	66

Another important issue with respect to sample size is the number and size of subgroups involved in the data analysis. It may be important to show an overall level of confusion, and then look more closely at consumers with a similar grouping characteristic. For example, if there is some question that older people would be more susceptible to confusion than younger people, sufficient numbers of consumers in the different age groups are needed. Similarly, if comparisons between males and females are important, the researcher would want to make sure the power within each subgroup was sufficient to determine if there was any intra-group differences.

Incomplete Questionnaires

A further practical consideration is the problem of incomplete questionnaires. It is not uncommon for a respondent to start answering the questions of a study, then decide not to finish the interview. If there is a self-completion part, some critical questions may be deliberately omitted by the respondent because he or she is judged to be irrelevant or too personal. Some questions may just be missed inadvertently. Sometimes these incomplete questionnaires are not useful because critical questions are not answered. In these cases, the entire questionnaire might have to be removed from the tabulation. This is a common problem in research, particularly in North America. A colleague received a frantic phone call from a data analysis company in Japan telling him that 6 percent to 7 percent of the questionnaires filled out by the American sample was not complete. The non-response from the matched Japanese sample was only 1 percent. The colleague had to tell the company not to worry, that 6 to 7 percent non-response was actually very good. Sample sizes should be sufficient to allow for up to ten percent deletion of possible incomplete questionnaires.

'Don't Know' Responses

"Don't know" responses are a peculiar problem. On one hand, "don't know" may reflect confusion; on the other hand, it may mean "don't care." "Don't know" may also reflect its literal meaning. The researcher may want to delete these responses or analyze them separately to avoid criticism and show conservatism in data analysis. By deleting persons who state they don't know, one is left with a sample of people who do have a certain perception of the problem at hand. They should represent people confident in their judgments. An alternative method might be for the researcher to tabulate the results in a manner that both includes and separates the "don't know" respondents to give a complete picture of the data analyses.

Summary

Given this theoretical background to the problem of sample size, the standards put forth by industry and government are that 300 subjects are needed for testing deceptive advertising. This is perceived to be a safe number of respondents as it should allow for non-responses, and for subgroup statistical analyses. A rule of thumb might be: The smaller the market and the more obvious the confusion, the smaller the sample needed; the larger the market and the less obvious the confusion, the larger the sample needed. Therefore, sample sizes of thirty to 1000 may be suitable, depending on the question under investigation.

TYPE OF SAMPLE

Perhaps even more important than the number of people sampled is the type of people used in the research. Decisions in FTC Act and Lanham Act cases dealing with consumer perceptions of advertising content have held that to determine conveyed meanings, there is no need for samples to: 1) be national probability samples; 2) include only those who use the product or have characteristics indicating the probability of such usage; or 3) include only those exposed to the media running the advertisement (Preston 1990). The explanation is that the perception of what a message is saying should not differ from one sort of person to another. The extent to which the above statements are generalizable to all consumer research does depend on the situation. There are cases where the courts have not been inclined to accept samples containing non-users of the product.

Users versus Purchasers

In most cases where the judicial system ignored or gave little weight to the study, its criticism concerned the type of people used in the samples. In *Jenkins Bros. v. Newman Hender & Co. Ltd.* (1961), the issue was a diamond-shaped design of a valve used in industrial settings. The plaintiff took a survey of plant supervisors and operation and maintenance personnel who were users but not necessarily purchasers of the product. The results of the survey were judged to be inconclusive and indicated that users of valves identified them by shape or type, rather than the design in question. This case is in contrast to *Price Pfister Inc. v. Mundo Corp. et al.* (1989), where the issue was also shape, but the product was faucets. In this case, purchasers of faucets were interviewed, and not just users. Faucets are likely to be bought by home builders, whereas the users of faucets are not likely to be purchasers unless they build their own homes.

Limited Users

In *Mead Data Central Inc. v. Toyota Motor Sales, U.S.A., Inc.* (1988), the issue was the name LEXIS vs. LEXUS. A survey showed that 76 percent of lawyers and 26 percent of accountants identified LEXIS as a computerized search service. Indeed, it is a service mainly used by lawyers. However, only 2 percent of the general public correctly identified it as such. The point is that the LEXUS car market was not limited to lawyers and accountants, but to the general public within a certain income bracket. Using a sample of lawyers and accountants to identify the name did not represent all potential car purchasers.

Unlikely Purchasers

To be more precise about potential purchasers one may have to identify past purchasers, intended purchasers, or those who might influence purchase decisions (Reiner 1983). Identifying these subtle differences in the sample might ward off criticism about the type of person used in the research. One of the most widely cited cases concerning inappropriate samples is *Amstar Corp. v. Domino's Pizza Inc.* (1980). Both sides presented research studies that were judged to be lacking. The court suggested that the relevant sample for purchasers of Domino's Pizzas would be single, college-age males. The court ruled that the perceptions of middle-aged females with respect to pizza, would lend no relevant information on which an expert could rely when testifying about marketing choices of potential purchasers of pizza products.

Specific Users

The complexity of the issue is exemplified in *Weight Watchers International Inc. v. The Stouffer Corp.* (1990). Weight Watchers alleged that Stouffers' advertising represented an endorsement by Weight Watchers of the Stouffer product. Weight Watchers had to prove that the public believed it had approved or endorsed Stouffer products. Stouffers' advertising did not use the Weight Watchers trademark to designate its own product, but instead used it on "compatibility advertising or advertising about the fit with a competitor's product or service." The judge found fault with the research of both sides in this case.

Both the defendant's and the plaintiff's research focused on individuals who bought and ate frozen food and/or who had tried to lose weight. The alleged problem was that neither survey focused on people who ate diet or low-calorie frozen foods, or even people who were trying to lose weight through dieting as opposed to exercise. Given this reasoning by the court, some of the respondents may not have been in the market for diet food of any kind and therefore the studies' samples were judged to be too broad.

The theoretical rationale is that respondents who are not potential customers may well be less likely than potential customers to be aware of and to make relevant distinctions when reading advertisements. The ability to make relevant decisions is crucial when what is being tested is the likelihood of confusion. The judge ruled that the research methodology was so flawed that he had no alternative but to personally assess the advertisements. Some judges do not appreciate the fact that a highly informed sample of one is never better at judging perception than a naive group of "average" consumers.

Summary

The type of people who constitute the universe in a trademark litigation study is defined in terms of the following characteristics (Sorensen 1983):

1. Relevance. The beliefs, perceptions, attitudes, and behaviors of the individuals are of interest to the case at hand. The subject in a consumer research study of brand imitation should be either a purchaser or user of the good or service. However, there are instances where the user may not be the purchaser or the purchaser may not be the user.

2. Accessibility. The relevant individuals should be available for an interview. It is not always necessary for a random probability sample to be used in consumer research.

3. Identifiable. The relevant individuals must be identified by certain characteristics that can be used to screen qualified respondents without alerting them to the purpose of the research.

4. Cooperation. The relevant individuals must permit themselves to be interviewed about the object of investigation in sufficient numbers.

The type of research used to detect brand imitation is based on marketing research and is likely to employ experimental methods as well as survey research methods.

CONSUMER RESEARCH

Although perfect research does not exist, the research carried out for litigation must be designed in a meticulous manner, with close attention to the legal logic to which the results of the study will be subjected. Standards for judicial research are supplied by Morgan (1990) and are adapted in Table 6.3.

Table 6.3
Guidelines for Conducting Research for Brand Imitation

1.   Sample Selection

   a)   Relevant respondents for the sample are those who might purchase, use, or have an
        opinion about the object of investigation.
   b)   Convenience and nonprobability sampling must be relevant respondents.
   c)   Sample size should be powerful enough to detect 20-30% confusion levels.

2.   Design of Questionnaire

   a)   Questions that appear to predispose respondents must be avoided.
   b)   Question wording must be direct, clear, and unambiguous.
   c)   Research questions must relate directly to the legal question being litigated.
   d)   Objective questions must include properly stated, complete sets of response scales.
   e)   Objective questions should be simple and elicit answers to one question at a time.
   f)   Questionnaires should be pretested to the relevant respondents to ensure the above
        conditions are met.

3.   Administration of Questionnaire

        Research designs may be devised in the context of normal marketplace conditions or
        normal test market conditions subject to the legal research questions being investigated.

4.   Interviewers' Qualifications and Techniques

   a)   Interviewers should not know the name of the organization sponsoring the research.
   b)   Interviewers should not know the purpose of the research project.
   c)   Interviewers must not be associated in any way with the litigants in the lawsuit.

5.   Data Analysis and Presentation

   a)   All data should be reported.
   b)   Data should be presented by simple frequencies before statistical analysis.

6.   Administration of Overall Project

   a)   The research administrator must be a recognized expert, based on peer review, in
        marketing research.
   b)   The research administrator must continuously and closely supervise all steps in the
        research project.
   c)   The research administrator must have minimum contact with and direction from attorneys.

Adapted from F. Morgan (1990), *Journal of Marketing, 54*, "Judicial Standards for
Survey Research: An Update and Guidelines," p. 63.

Action Is Better than Words

The type of data collected depends on the issue. However,
consumer research data usually fare best when they describe
particular behaviors rather than just perceptions. This is especially so if monetary damages are sought. When a company

wants to be compensated for lost sales or potential loss of sales, there must be some direct evidence that the loss of these sales was due to the imitator product.

Behavior is also important because one of the primary factors considered in passing-off cases is confusion. However, courts are also said to realize that obtaining evidence of confusion may be extremely difficult, so therefore evidence of actual confusion is not necessary (Allen 1993). One of the reasons cited for the difficulty of obtaining confusion evidence is that most consumers do not complain about purchasing an imitator product they did not intend to purchase. This is because the imitator product is usually so much lower in price. Another reason for not returning the imitator product is that consumers are reluctant to admit that they made a mistake or were deceived in their purchase. Therefore, controlled research studies are needed to measure the extent to which the choice was due to imitation.

Obtaining data on choices or selections with imitators is ideal, but does not always provide complete information on the case. Even when consumers are observed selecting the imitator over the original, it is important to know why that choice occurred. If a consumer believes two brands to be similar in appearance, it does not necessarily mean that he or she was motivated to purchase one brand instead of the other because of its appearance. For example, in a study that found that customers bought a brand with a name similar to the original, the judge ruled that confusion was not necessarily demonstrated (*Squirt Co. v. Seven-Up Co. 1980*). To demonstrate confusion, the judge wanted evidence that explicitly identified why that brand was bought (Crespi 1987). Therefore, an investigation of motives may be critical.

A valid and useful motivation survey could be based more on investigation of whether the trademark generates specific attitudes and beliefs about the product's attributes. Measures are then taken to determine whether those specific attitudes and beliefs cause the consumer to select the product. In *Zippo Mfg. Co. v. Rogers Imports Inc.* (1963), the final measurement of these attitudes and beliefs was the choice of the product. At the end of the research interview, the respondents were offered their choice of a Zippo lighter or an imitator brand. The original was preferred by more than two to one, and the court noted this as proof of the motivational aspect of the expectations formed by the original brand (Leiser and Schwartz 1983).

TECHNIQUES FOR EVALUATING BRAND IMITATION

Flash Card Technique

Pre-Testing for Infringement. Researchers may carry out very simple pre-tests to generate data that might indicate whether more sophisticated controlled studies are worth pursuing. The flash card technique is one example of a pre-test for infringement of logo and/or trademark confusion of products. A series of three-by-five-inch or five-by-eight-inch cards are prepared so that each displays a trademark, and possibly the term describing the goods to which it is applied, such as Ivory soap. The number of different trademarks may range from ten to fifteen. Among the series of cards is one bearing the trademark thought to be infringed upon. These cards are shown to a convenience sample, usually a college class or church group. Each person is given several seconds to read each card. Somewhat later, perhaps one hour, the same group is shown a series of similar cards in which there are several repeats (five to eight) from the original series, but in which the original trademark card is substituted by the accused trademark. The respondents are asked at the end of the second series to write down all the trademarks they can recall as having been shown in both the first and second series.

If a critical percentage of the sample indicates that the infringer's logo was shown to them in the first series, there is some evidence that the two marks are subject to confusion. A further form of testing for confusion might then be warranted, as this form of testing is artificial and far removed from the marketplace. The pre-test sample might not even be composed of relevant purchasers. While flash card testing is good for specific logos or trademarks, it is not a recommended method for testing infringement of the Gestalt or overall look of the article.

Using Photographs

Sometimes it is difficult to show respondents the object of investigation in the way they naturally see it in the environment. Logos or trade dress involving outdoor signs or buildings may cause particular problems. In *Exxon Corp. v. Texas Motor Exchange of Houston Inc.* (1980), the question was infringement of the logo. It was thought that consumers would believe Texxon was associated with Exxon. Exxon argued that the double x identified its company alone. To test the difference between Texxon and Texon, subjects were shown a photograph of the Texxon sign and asked questions similar to the following:

1. Does anything come to mind when looking at this sign?
    (If Yes):
    What is it?
    (Record verbatim)
2. What was there about the sign that made you say
    that?
    (Probe fully)
3. (If no company name mentioned): What is the first company that comes to mind when you look at this sign?
    (Record name exactly as respondent states it)
4. What was there about the sign that made you mention (the company)?
    (Clarify and probe fully). (Boal 1983: 414)

The beauty of these questions lies in the fact that they do not lead the respondent to give any one answer. Perhaps the most informative question is the last one. It allows the respondent to articulate what led to any possible confusion or what caused the confusion, if it existed. These questions do not directly ask the respondent about association, sponsorship, or connection; the respondent makes the connection in his or her own mind.

Tachistoscope Research

A basic method of determining threshold levels of perception is with a tachistoscope (t-scope). This device is similar to a slide projector but is capable of extremely rapid exposure rates. The subject views the screen, watches for the stimulus, and then reports what he or she has just seen. The rate of exposure is varied until there is detection of the stimulus. In cognitive psychology it is used to determine the level at which a stimulus may be consciously identified.

In marketing research, t-scopes are used to assess a product's shelf visibility and distinctiveness (Valerio 1992), or confusion of brands for the same product. It has been used to test outdoor poster recognition and comprehension by exposing viewers to only fractions of seconds of each poster. It has also been used at speeds that simulate a reader flipping through a magazine to measure the extent to which messages are communicated, or attention is captured (Day 1974).

T-scope studies of the criteria of limited attention are important to manufacturers, as courts have previously rejected the results on the basis that respondents had too much time to reflect on their decisions. The notion of the hurried consumer scanning the shelves (see Chapter 2) is very difficult to reproduce in a natural setting. The best way to guarantee limited attention is through the use of a tachistoscope.

Case Study: Oil of Olay. In determining product confusion, the t-scope has been used in cases such as Oil of Olay (see Smith et al. 1983 for a complete description of the case). This beauty product was sold in a pink and black package, in which a Madonna-like head is featured in a center cartouche. The cartouche is created by a "reverse" printing technique. Oil of Olay was extremely successful, with sales of over $50 million in 1977. Soon after, the marketplace became flooded with private label "knock-offs" of Oil of Olay, all in pink and black dress, with names like "Oil of Beauty" and "Oil of Life."

To test for consumer confusion, a number of competitive packages and a "knock-off" were included on a display shelf. Oil of Olay lotion was not on the shelf, but one of the infringing packages was. Subjects were then shown pictures of the store shelves at timed intervals starting at one-twelfth of a second. Respondents were asked, "What brands did you see?" Depending on the package being tested, a substantial number of respondents misidentified the stimulus product as Oil of Olay.

This test was used in a preliminary way because it helped identify the major package infringers. These laboratory tests may not be final proof of likelihood of confusion, but they provide data to the plaintiff or the expert witness for the basis of opinion. Because this is a basic industry technique used to assess identification, it is also an appropriate tool to assess misidentification. Defendants had a very difficult time explaining why people, sitting four feet from the defendant's "Oil of Beauty" lotion, would identify it as Oil of Olay.

Previous courtroom criticism of this technique concerns the precision in determining the percentage of customer confusion in the marketplace. Because each person's threshold for identification may be slightly different, it is difficult to say what exposure time is the correct one for accurate identification of the objects in question. The data were thought best used for demonstration or anecdotal evidence because the data will attract the court's attention and provide a good basis for expert testimony. The protocol is quick and relatively inexpensive (Smith et al. 1983).

Determining Exposure Rates. Studies by Kapferer and Thoenig (1991) and Kapferer (1993) sought to develop standards for exposure times in t-scope tests for courtroom evidence. The aim of their work was to show that there is risk of brand confusion among consumers, whether the copycat product is presented in isolation or with the original. The exposure of one brand in isolation is a common in-store situation. Because many copycat brands are created by big retailers, they receive the most visible spots on the shelves. The original brands may get less prominent spots or perhaps are not distributed at all. Thus, exposure in isolation is of interest.

In the Kapferer and Thoenig (1991) study, consumers were exposed by tachistoscope either to the copycat brand in isolation or paired with the original at exposures of 1/125th, 1/60th, 1/15th, 1/4th, 1/2, and one second. The two types of data were collected to represent different types of in-store experiences.

Consumers viewed four different products and were exposed to each of the original and copycat brands in isolation six times. After each exposure they were asked three questions: 1) What did you see? 2) What do you think you saw? and 3) What does it represent? The product category and the name of the brand were coded. The results of the study showed that some brands were confused with their copycat brands up to 42 percent of the time. An index of confusion was proposed where:

$$I = \frac{\text{\% identifying brand as a copy}}{\text{\% identifying brand as original}}$$

In some cases the index of confusion showed little variation over the different exposure times, indicating that a very long detailed look at the copycat brand was necessary to be sure it was not the original.

The methodology in the Kapferer (1993) paper is similar, but the research concerns only reactions to brands in isolation. The study found that for most imitators, the highest rate of confusion (perceiving the national brand when the copy was shown) does not take place at the highest speed, but after some exposure time, either 1/15th or 1/4th of a second. Furthermore, the variance in the rates of confusion for different products and consumers is wide, ranging from zero to 42 percent. Also, the rates of confusion do not decrease rapidly with time. At one full second of exposure, 22 percent to 24 percent of consumers confused certain brands with their imitators.

Summary. Tachistoscopes can also be replaced by computer screens. The same procedure is followed, but subjects see the images on the computer rather than on a screen. Computer-assisted design programs have now made this possible. It is also possible to vary the design, color, and brand name through the computer images, to determine how the imitator brand can be changed so as not to be confused with the original. This type of research is very controlled and offers a precise measure of imitation.

Consumer Reaction Tests

Sometimes the best test for determination of brand imitation involves a consumer reaction test outside of the context of a purchase. There are many types of consumer reaction tests, each designed for a specific purpose. A consumer reaction test is not a survey of public opinion. Rather, it involves the direct exposure of an object to consumers, and then measures their reactions to or thoughts about what they have just seen. The purpose is not to measure their reactions to the image in their memory, but to measure the direct impression of the object as they see it. The brand impression may be measured in isolation or in the context of other brands.

This type of testing is very important in cases involving alleged infringement of package design, association, or sponsorship. Different problems call for different methods. For example, advertising, which may be the subject of a passing-off inquiry, may be presented to consumers under artificial conditions. Consumers are exposed to the advertisement in isolation rather than in the context of regular television viewing in their home. After viewing the advertisement in a test theater or a shopping mall format, consumers are asked questions about what they have just seen.

This format would likely cause respondents to attend to the advertisement very closely, and thus they would be more aware of the content of the advertisement. Consumers should therefore comprehend the message better than they would if viewing it under natural conditions. This type of testing is conservative in that there may be fewer people confused because of their greater attention. It is likely that more evidence of confusion would be found under inattentive but natural viewing. Therefore controlled attentive viewing is a strong rather than a weak test for confusion because it underestimates the number of people confused under natural viewing conditions.

The Federal Trade Commission has identified this type of consumer reaction test as the preferred type of extrinsic evidence for determining conveyance in advertising research because it is more direct than other types of research, such as calling people after an advertisement had aired (Preston 1989a; 1989b). This does not mean that "day-after recall" tests are totally invalid, but only that their failure to show conveyance of any confusion does not conclusively mean that none occurred. If confusion is found under natural conditions, more conservative tests might not be necessary.

Case Study: Robin Hood. Another example of reaction test questionnaires and labels is used to determine association or confusion of source. In *International Milling Co. v. Robin Hood Popcorn Co.* (1956), the issue was that Robin Hood Flour was thought to be extremely well known to the public. Another company produced and sold Robin Hood Popcorn. The flour mill undertook to prove that consumers thought the two products came from the same source. To test this premise, 512 households were shown wrappers or tags from six products with the name of the producer removed from the label or package. Six products were used so that the respondents would not guess which product was the focus of the research. The products were: Carnation milk, Ivory soap, Robin Hood popcorn, Baker's chocolate, Log Cabin syrup, and Monarch green beans.

Respondents were shown the wrappers or labels one at a time and asked: "What is the name of the company that makes___?" They were then shown the labels again, one at a time, and asked "Have you ever bought___?" The final but critical question was: "If you can think of any other products put out by each of these companies, please name them." The labels were again shown one at a time to the respondent. If a significant number of consumers mentioned flour in response to the last question, that was a good indication of confusion of source of the product (Pattishall 1959). The main parts of the questionnaire are reproduced in Exhibit 6.2.

There are some important points to be made with respect to the questionnaire design of Exhibit 6.2. First, the questionnaire should be short, but not so short that the key issue is obvious. Second, it should not trigger any particular response to the key question. Third, it should be designed to answer a specific question about confusion. Fourth, the questionnaire should hold the interest of the respondent and ensure that the answers obtained are given seriously. Fifth, it should be written in a non-technical manner with words easily understood by those at a high school level. Last, the results should be presented as a simple tabulation of percentage confused.

Of the above points, the one most likely to cause courtroom arguments is the accusation of leading questions. The perception of a question as being leading is likely to be a subjective matter. It is best to be as conservative as possible, perhaps designing a questionnaire that might just as likely be used by the opposing company.

Shopping for the Product

In-Store Coupon Test. To test for the level of confusion between two brands in a retail environment, cooperation might be obtained from one or more retail establishments to carry out a field experiment. The potential advantages the retailer receives would be increased store traffic by the research participants and awareness of shelf stocking by the researchers.

Exhibit 6.2
Consumer Reaction Test for Origin of Manufacturer

Q. 1. What is the name of the company that makes (show pictures).

CARNATION?	_____
IVORY?	_____
ROBIN HOOD/	_____
LOG CABIN?	_____
MONARCH?	_____

Q. 2. Have you ever bought

	Yes	No	Don't Remember
CARNATION?	____	____	____
IVORY?	____	____	____
ROBIN HOOD?	____	____	____
LOG CABIN?	____	____	____
MONARCH?	____	____	____

Q. 3. If you can think of any other products put out by each of these companies, please name them.

CARNATION	_____
IVORY	_____
ROBIN HOOD	_____
LOG CABIN	_____
MONARCH	_____

Adapted from B. W. Pattishall (1959), Reaction test evidence in trade identity cases. *Trademark Reporter, Vol. 49*, 160–61.

The researcher sets up shelves in the store by placing the competing brand on the shelf alongside the target brand. There may be several versions of the placement: 1) the competitor may be directly to the left or right of the target; 2) the competitor may be separated by other brands; 3) the competitor may be directly to the right of the target; and 4) the competitor may be above or below the target. The reason for the different placings is to counterbalance any positioning bias. It is widely accepted that the position of a product on store shelves can influence sales. For example, Brand A will sell better than Brand B if A is at eye level and B is at ankle level.

Aisle-end displays and the number of facings also affect sales. More subtle positional biases (such as right-handed people choosing the brand on the right because of ease of reach) are less obvious, but the possibility can be guarded against by rotation of positions. Each of the different positions can then be used to determine if different results are based on positioning and to eliminate the possible criticism of positional bias.

In shopping for the product (Boal 1973), the consumer is intercepted outside the store and given coupons for three products, valid for that day only. The coupons are usually at a third discount, such as one dollar off a three dollar purchase. If the purchase is usually made by the look or Gestalt of the item, the respondents are shown pictures of the brands the coupons represent. If the original brand has regular discount coupons bearing the brand's mark prominently, they may also be used. The consumer is always given two or three products to shop for so as not to direct his or her attention to the focal product. The shopper is then allowed to enter the store and the brands purchased are recorded at the check-out counter.

This type of research works well when the brand name under study is not widely known by the consumer, but the look of the brand is very distinctive. For example in *Hartford House Ltd. v. Hallmark Cards Inc.* (1986) where the overall look or Gestalt of the card was well known, but perhaps not the brand name, this might have been a very good test to determine the level of confusion among consumers.

Case Study: St. Ives Shampoo. Consumer shopping was used in the St. Ives shampoo and conditioner case, where consumers recognized the trade dress but not the brand name (*Ives Laboratories Inc. v. Darby Drug Co., Inc.*, 1982). The products were sold in containers through which the color of the ingredients could be seen. The shampoo and conditioner bottles were branded together by plastic wrap to form a twin pack, and a promotional tag was placed on top of one of the bottles. The bottle had the trademark "Swiss Formula" printed vertically on the left side of the principal display panel. Imitators in the market used the same twin pack concept with a plastic wrap. They were called "Salon Formula" or "European Formula".

In using the shopping format test, up to 40 percent of the shoppers bought the competitors' goods after being shown the St.

Ives picture before entering the store. That is persuasive evidence for confusion. Because this test demonstrates actual consumer confusion and does not attempt to quantify the likelihood of confusion, much lower percentages of consumers might need to select the "wrong" product for persuasive evidence. In *RJR Foods Inc. v. White Rock Corp.* (1978), 15 percent to 20 percent of the shoppers purchasing the wrong brand was deemed reliable evidence of confusion. It should be noted that this is a strongly conservative test in that it involves a typical consumer setting. Consumer shopping tests are best done for inexpensive, non-durable products.

Natural Purchase Situation

Sometimes consumers intend to buy a certain Brand A but once in the retail environment, they encounter a Brand B so similar that they purchase it. The purchase could be a mistake or it could be made because Brand B is cheaper and looks just like Brand A. The consumer may just disregard the confusion. This scenario was found in an initial study of brand imitators: "I didn't realize it until I got home, but was too embarrassed to take it back. I used it. It was just a frozen vegetable" (Levy and Rook 1981: 192).

If Brand B meets the consumer's expectations and is sufficiently lower in price (partly due to the lower costs of being an imitator), the consumer may switch to the mistaken brand. In these cases the consumer is transferring his or her beliefs and attitudes from the original product to the brand imitator because of the similarity or generalization of the two brands. The question in such circumstances is not whether consumers can discriminate between the two products on some secondary cue, but rather, whether the positive attitudes that have been linked to the first brand are generalized to the second brand in a way that leads to buying behavior (Miaoulis and D'Amato 1978).

Case Study: Tic Tacs. An example of measuring this transfer of beliefs and attitudes from Brand A to the alleged infringer, Brand B, is demonstrated in the investigation of Tic Tac Mints versus Dynamints and Mightymints. The case is given in detail in Miaoulis and D'Amato (1978). The premise of the investigation was that consumers have a distinct conception of Tic Tac's taste and product benefits and that this image is immediately triggered by the visual impact of the product, the package, and the display.

Consumer surveys were conducted in two cities where the infringing brands were not yet sold but where the original brand was well established. Tic Tacs were replaced by the imitator brands in drug, variety, and grocery outlets in Detroit and New Jersey. Consumers were intercepted after purchasing the test brand (198 interviews in Detroit and 131 in New Jersey), but before they had an opportunity to open the package and taste the product. The basic question asked in this research was: "Do people, through the visual impact of the product [the plastic box with the visual configuration of the pellets within], anticipate obtaining the same end benefits and the same experiences that they would with Tic Tac?" Because consumers had not previously experienced or heard of Dynamints or Mightymints, product expectations could be taken to stem from the visual aspects of the product.

The specific questions asked of the respondents were:

1. What do you expect this product to be like?
2. What made you believe it would be like this?
3. Do you believe this product would be like any other product on the market?
4. Which one or ones is it like?
5. Do you believe these two products are made by the same company?
6. Why do you feel this way?

At no point during the questionnaire was Tic Tac mentioned by name unless the brand was introduced by the respondent. When the responses to the questions were tabulated, the purchasers overwhelmingly referred to Tic Tac brand. In an out-of-court settlement, the packaging for Dynamints was changed to decrease the visual impact of the scrambled product configuration, and Mightymints withdrew from the market.

The study described above is slightly different from the previously presented in-store shopping scenario because consumers are not instructed to buy the product before entering the store. The problems in gathering data of this type are numerous. First, just obtaining an adequate sample that naturally purchases the product could take a long time. It is rare that a substantial quantity of a product is sold, in a given time frame, in a self-serve environment. If the goods are not sold in a self-serve environment, the practical difficulties of conducting the study under controlled conditions are immense. It may also be a problem to obtain the co-operation of store owners and managers, who will benefit little, if at all, from the study. The benefits of this method are also its weaknesses. It represents a real purchase situation, yet there is no control over the frequency of people participating.

Signal Detection Theory

Signal detection theory is one of the greatest successes of mathematical psychology (Wickens 1991). It was originally developed to measure a weak signal in a noisy environment. An individual must often decide whether some condition is present or absent. Most of the time the alternatives are obvious and the evidence is clear. However, sometimes the alternatives may be distinct, but the evidence is ambiguous. For example, is the original brand present or absent? The alternatives are distinct, but the other brands may look so similar that the evidence is ambiguous. Therefore, signal detection theory is useful in quantifying the identification of certain target brands among the other competing brands, or in measuring the amount of brand confusion for brands within the same product category.

In a signal detection experiment, the subject experiences two types of trials. In some trials only the competing brands or background environment are present. In the other type of trial, the target brand or signal is added to the overall brand environment. In both types of trials the observer is asked to detect the presence of the original brand. Detection of a signal is known as a "hit." Astute observers of distinctive brands have high hit rates; poor observers, or the presentation of confusingly similar brands, yield low hit rates. Unfortunately, the hit rate is not a true summary of the situation or a good way to indicate the distinctiveness of the brand. The problem lies in the overall look of the available brands or the context of the choice.

To resolve the background problem, it is important *not* to report the presence of a target brand (signal) when one is not there, a type of error known as a "false alarm." If the brand is correctly identified

Figure 6.1
Signal Detection Matrix for Original Brand

Respondent's Answer

		Yes	No
	Yes	Hits	Misses
Original Present	**No**	"Indication of Imitation" (false alarm)	"Indication of Uniqueness" (correct rejection)

85 percent of the time when it is there, that may be a good hit rate. However, if the brand is identified 60 percent of the time when it is not actually there, the rate of false alarms indicates a lot of confusion about the presence of the target brand. The brand is likely to be undistinctive and easily confused with another. Researching the problem of confusion must take into account both hits and false alarms to get a complete picture of possible brand imitation.

Methodology. The procedure for signal detection of brand imitation is adapted from Donovan (1987). Respondents are shown pairs of slides projected on a screen. The first slide contains a matrix of brands and the second slide features just one brand. Thus, two types of slides are prepared: the matrix slides consisting of the majority of the brands and the target slides consisting of only one brand. The number of target slides might represent the major competitors and the object of investigation. If, for example, four brands are chosen as the target brands, the original and imitator brands at issue are tested along with two other competitors. The two other competitors should be distinct to determine the extent of brand differentiation. Testing more than the target brand also helps camouflage the purpose of the research to the participating consumers.

The results obtained for each target brand, as represented by Figure 6.1, are based on the possible combinations of correct responses (yes or no) and the person's actual answer (yes or no). The hits represent the proportion of times that the target brand was correctly detected when it was present in the preceding matrix slide. This measure gives an indication of how well the brand stands out among its competitors.

The misses represent the proportion of times that respondents thought the brand was not in the matrix when it actually was. The proportion of misses may be taken to indicate the overall similarity within the product category, or how poorly the target brand stands out from other brands. The false alarms represent the proportion of times that respondents thought the target brand was in the preceding matrix when it actually was not. This measure provides an indication of the degree of confusion about each brand or how easily it is mistaken for another brand.

The correct rejections represent the proportion of times that respondents correctly determined that the target brand was not in the preceding matrix. This gives a good indication of the uniqueness of the target brand. The issue here is to compare the detectability of the alleged imitating brand with the original brand. The first step is to compute the detectability of the original brand on the shelf to get a base rate of identification. It could be that all brands in the marketplace look similar. If the original brand stands out and is not confused with the competitors, the results in Figure 6.2 might occur.

In this case, the original brand can be easily detected and is not readily confused with other competitors. In the following case, depicted in Figure 6.3, the original brand is easily identified, but also confused with competitors. By establishing this base rate for the original brand, all other results can be compared with it.

To measure the imitation level of the imitator brand, the matrix would contain the original brand and the target slide would contain the imitator brand. This would yield a slightly different matrix, as shown in Figure 6.4. The pattern of responses under false alarms and hits might indicate the relationship of the imitator to other brands in the marketplace. The false alarms and hits would indicate the extent to which the infringing brand is similar to or different from the original brand. The original brand is not used in the matrix because the issue is not how well the imitator is detected, but how similar the imitator is to the original brand.

Figure 6.2
Signal Detection Matrix of Distinctive Brands

Respondent's Answer

		Yes	*No*	Total
Original Brand	*Present*	75 - 90%	10 - 25%	100%
	Absent	10 - 25%	75 - 90%	100%

Figure 6.3
Signal Detection Matrix of Non-Distinctive Brands

Respondent's Answer

		Yes	*No*	Total
Original Brand	*Present*	75 - 90%	10 - 25%	100%
	Absent	50%	50%	100%

Figure 6.4
Signal Detection Matrix for Imitator Brand

Respondent's Answer for Detection of Original

		Yes	*No*
Imitator Brand	*Present*	"Indication of Imitation" (confusion)	"Indication of Uniqueness" (correct rejection)
	Absent	False Alarm	Hits

Figure 6.5
Task for Signal Detection of Brands

```
Exposure 1
                                    0  0  0
       (matrix slide of brands)     T  0  0
                                    0  0  0
       - one second


Exposure 2

       (target slide)                  T

       - three seconds
```

TASK - Was the target present or not?

The procedure, as used by Donovan Research (1987), involves gathering consumer reactions of three to four respondents at a time in a consumer testing facility. Each respondent is presented with each target slide six times, three times with the target brand present in the matrix slide and three times with the target absent. The position of the target brand in the matrix slide is randomized over the three slides. The basic task is represented in Figure 6.5. The total number of slides is six times the number of target brands. It seems reasonable that the original, the imitator, and perhaps two other brands would be chosen for filler, giving twenty-four slides to show the respondents. The order of presentation of the slides of the imitator and the original should be represented with equal frequency in the first third, middle third, and final third of the trials. Within each of these segments, presentation order should be random.

Prior to the first trial, a demonstration of the task should be completed by the interviewer. The respondents should then complete two practice trials themselves under timed conditions to fully understand and familiarize themselves with the procedure. The instructions and scoring for this task might be as follows:

The first slide showing the nine brands will only be shown on the screen for one second. If it is shown for any longer, the task becomes too easy and people get all the questions right. Sometimes the brand shown in the second slide will have been one of the nine shown in the first slide and sometimes the brand shown in the second slide will not have been one of the nine shown in the first slide.

For each pair of slides, I want you to make your *best possible guess* even though you are not sure. It turns out that people always do much better than they think when they take their best possible guess. For this reason, I want you to tick either "Yes" or "No" on *each* occasion depending on whether you think the brand shown in the second slide was one of those shown in the first slide or not. You are not allowed to say that you "don't know." Just take your best possible guess as soon as you see the second slide.

Do you have any questions?

The results would be tabulated and comparisons made between the scores obtained for the original brand and the imitator. The number of subjects needed for this test is not large as each subject has multiple exposures. The important point is to include relevant consumers and allow for sufficient numbers of any subgroups that might be important, such as age or sex. The minimum number for any subgroup would be about thirty. A sample of 100 would allow for two or three subgroups.

QUESTIONS FOR SPONSORSHIP

Sometimes testing for association of two objects is not enough. The question may be whether product A is approved and endorsed by company or product B. For example, in *Ideal Toy Corp. v. Kenner et al.* (1977), a finding of general association that the toys in question looked like characters from the movie "Star Wars" or reminded respondents of the movie was not enough for the courts. They ruled that this association did not mean that a purchaser thinks the toys are derived from the movie or sponsored by the movie (Boal 1983).

Getting people to freely describe sponsorship, endorsements, or approval is extremely difficult. Therefore it is usually best to ask respondents these questions directly. The National Football League has been successful in presenting evidence which showed that it did not sponsor or endorse state lottery tickets (*National Football League v. Governor of the State of Delaware* 1977), or clothing (*National Football League Properties Inc. v. Wichita Falls Sportswear Inc.* 1982). In the first case, the respondents were asked whether they agreed that the lottery was conducted with the authorization of the teams. In the second case the respondents were asked directly if the company producing the clothing had to obtain authorization or sponsorship to make the clothing. Then they were asked from whom the authorization was obtained.

In the situations of sponsorship or association, it is best to divide the question into smaller parts that address specific issues. For example, instead of asking, "Do you think these two products are made by the same or different producers?" it would be better to ask, "Do you think these two products are made by the same producers?" and then "Do you think these two products are made by different producers?" These questions can also be given as statements with Likert scales, a type of scaling where the respondents are presented with a series of statements, rather than questions, and asked to indicate the degree to which they agree or disagree, usually on a five point scale. By asking the question in two parts one is able to get both positive and negative responses. One question acts as a balance or reliability check for the other. The two questions should also be counterbalanced by sometimes asking the positive question first and sometimes asking the negative question first. By counterbalancing the questions, both positive and negative ideas are equally introduced and therefore any perceived conditioning of the respondent should be reduced to random error.

Case Study: Paul Hogan. Examples of these two points are found in an Australian case, *Hogan and Another v. Koala Dundee* (1988). Both sides presented research to determine if consumers thought certain clothing sold by the Koala Dundee shop was associated or licensed by Paul Hogan. The applicant's study, performed by a marketing research firm, showed potential customers three items that were sold in the respondent's shop: a shopping bag, a T-shirt, and a hat. The consumers were asked five questions with respect to each item:

1. What does this mean to you?
2. Do you associate this with any person or thing?
3. Which person or thing came to mind?
4. Do you think that the person or thing which came to mind has any involvement with the (bag) (T-shirt) (hat)?
5. What do you think that involvement is?

In contrast, the respondent's study was carried out by the shop's employees and did not involve any specific offending merchandise. The shop's customers were given a questionnaire and asked to tick yes or no to the following questions:

When you saw our shop and our goods on display:
1. Did you wonder whether our goods are sold under an agreement with or by licence of Paul Hogan or those who made the film "Crocodile Dundee?"
2. Did you wonder whether our goods are sold with the sponsorship or approval of Paul Hogan or those who made the film "Crocodile Dundee?"

The applicant's questionnaire did not lead to any specific answer. The respondent's questions were leading in that they put the idea of sponsorship in the mind of the person reading the question. This is ironic as the respondent should want to avoid this type of answer.

There were a few other flaws in the market research in this case. First, in the applicant's research, although the hat, shopping bag, and T-shirt should have been rotated in the order of presentation to the consumers, they apparently were not. The criticism was that in showing the hat first, the results could be biased in the favor of the applicant.

Second, the importance of using professionally trained interviewers who are naive to the reasons for the data collection is also apparent in this case. In the respondent's survey, done by members of the store staff, 8 percent of customers gave an affirmative answer to one interviewer and 25 percent of customers gave an affirmative answer to another interviewer. Therefore, substantial bias may be attributable to the person collecting the data.

Summary. It is important to separate the questions of association, sponsorship, or endorsement. Just because respondents feel two objects are associated does not necessarily mean that they feel one party sponsors or endorses the other. Therefore, questions about sponsorship should be separate from questions of association. Questions should also be asked in rotating order to avoid the possibility that the responses from the first question will affect responses to later questions.

QUALITATIVE RESEARCH AS EVIDENCE

No matter how well a consumer reaction test is designed or a consumer survey is prepared and documented, the courts might not have the expertise, confidence, or experience to independently evaluate its worth. Although the social science researcher and the courts are concerned with establishing the truth, they operate under very different definitions, precepts, and procedures (Crespi 1987). Social scientists establish the hypothesis question to be answered and then gather data to support or reject the premise. Their work is reviewed by their peers and evaluated by the methods used to collect and analyze data, as well as underlying theories. The published work represents a premise with evidence to be scrutinized.

The legal system starts with a point of contention. The two parties present evidence that will offer support only to their own point of view. It is up to the court to decide whose evidence is better. In this process, each side tries to discredit the other's evidence. The process of discrediting can be irrelevant to uncovering the truth, but each side is paid to win, not to be objective.

Furthermore, the courts treat every case as individual and specific. The ways the courts apply research findings and the criteria they use for accepting the data differ significantly from the "generalizable" world of the social scientist. Judges, who are the final decision makers, often do not have the expertise to adequately evaluate sample sizes and procedures. Testimony that specifies surrounding facts and circumstances is highly valued evidence in aiding the decision. This is also why consumer research can be enhanced with anecdotal and direct testimony, rather than being relied upon as the primary basis for reaching a verdict (Crespi 1987).

This arena of confrontations between paid experts is mostly decided by non-scientists—a jury and/or judge, who usually have no idea what the results of a t-test might signify. The decisions of cases are sometimes based on the impression or credibility of the opposing experts in direct testimony and under cross-examination rather than scientific testing.

Since impressions are so relevant and important, it is supportive to bring the numbers to life. Individual witnesses' uncontradicted evidence as to what they thought they said or bought can make a vivid impression in the courtroom (*A & M Pet Products Inc. v. Pieces Inc.* 1989). The ascertaining and parading of consumers as witnesses in the courtroom is a costly and tedious task. Furthermore, both sides can easily produce individual witnesses to support their point of view; however, getting individual respondents who participated in the consumer test to testify undermines the confidentiality of the respondent. It could grossly decrease the response rate if subjects knew there was a possibility they would be served with a subpoena to testify in court.

Alternative methods of bringing the data to life involve the use of videotapes. Because judges and juries have little or no experience with consumer research, videotaping the procedure followed in consumer reaction tests is most informative. Focus groups might be beneficial in cases involving secondary meaning, advertising, defamation, or the dilution of trademarks. Videotaping reactions from a dozen people giving free-flowing ideas and emotions lends a vitality to the evidence that drab numbers on a page can never do.

The importance of qualitative methods to support and enhance quantitative data is exemplified in *Grotian et al. v. Steinway & Sons* (1975). In this case, the quantitative data showed that 8 1/2 percent of consumers were confused as to the origin of the pianos, one of the lowest percentages in trademark infringement cases. However, detailed tape-recorded interviews of purchasers of Steinweg pianos were accepted to show the tendency of these consumers to believe Steinweg pianos to be the German-made Steinway ones.

EVIDENCE FROM SECONDARY SOURCES

In the 1942 movie "Miracle on 34th Street," the judge was put in the agonizing position of ruling on whether Kris Kringle was Santa Claus. The defendant had the clever idea of delivering all the mail stored at the post office that was addressed to Santa Claus to the courtroom. The judge stated that, if the United States Post Office identified Kris Kringle as Santa Claus, then that was proof enough for the courts.

The same evidence of misdirected mail, telephone calls, or other real mistakes is useful anecdotal evidence to back up statistical data. These types of occurrences show actual confusion about the source of the goods. It is a mistake to rely solely on this kind of evidence for establishing consumer confusion because there is no control over gathering the data. Hence, the courts might think these data are a result of carelessness rather than the imitative nature of the competing product or service under scrutiny.

Nonetheless, companies should keep track of wrong numbers by telephone logs, noting the time and nature of the call (*IMS Ltd. v. International Medical Systems Inc.* 1986; *Wells Fargo & Co. v. Wells Fargo Construction Co.* 1985). Notation of mail addressed correctly but intended for the other company may also be invaluable in the courtroom (*Harlequin Enterprises Ltd. v. Gulf & Western Corp.* 1981; *Purofied Down Products Corp. v. Puro Down International of New Jersey Corp.* 1982).

Advertising that depicts the wrong product is another form of secondary data (*Parkdale Custom Built Furniture Proprietary Limited v. Puxu Proprietary Limited* 1981–1982; *Smith v. Sturm, Ruger & Co. Inc.* 1985). In these cases retailers ran advertisements that showed one brand, but clearly labeled it as the competitors. In some of these cases the retailer might request reimbursement for running an advertisement from the competitor rather than from the manufacturer who was mislabeled (*Jockey International Inc. v. Burkhard* 1975). Retailers may also send coupons for redemption to the wrong manufacturer (*Glamorene Products Corp. v. Boyle-Midway Inc.* 1975; *Helene Curtis Industries Inc. v. Church & Dwight Co. Inc.* 1977). Advertising that mistakenly promotes one item as another may be very important in the courtroom.

FLAWS JUDGED TO DISCREDIT RESEARCH

It may be best for researchers to imagine themselves working for the opposing party while designing the research. It is always best to be as conservative as possible in one's research approach for the courtroom. The results from consumer research studies that seemed to be liberal in their approach or were deemed flawed by bias are often heavily discounted by the courts despite their being carried out by experts. For example, in *General Motors Corporation v. Cadillac Marine and Boat Co.* (1964), a study that showed a 22 percent level of apparent confusion between Cadillac boats and Cadillac cars was given no weight by the court. This was mainly due to a question determined to be leading: "Will you please name anything else you think is put out by the same company?" Similarly, in *Sears, Roebuck and Co. v. Allstate Driving School Inc.* (1964), the court gave little or no weight to a seemingly biased survey, even though 49.8 percent of the respondents were confused between Allstate Driving School and Allstate automobile insurance (Robin and Barnaby 1973).

In *Amstar Corp. v. Domino's Pizza Inc.* (1980), the court attacked the marketing research of both parties, finding that the samples in each study failed to include a fair sampling of purchasers most likely to partake of the other party's product. Of the ten cities in which the plaintiff's study was conducted, eight had no Domino's Pizza outlets, and the outlets in the remaining two had been open for less than three months. The trial court discounted the defendant's research because it was conducted on the premises of Domino's Pizza outlets and therefore thought not to examine a proper sample. The questioning procedures used were also judged to be improper.

It is advisable not to use informal surveys that use respondents not naive to the issues. While this last point may seem odd, it is not unusual for law firms to do this. The problem is that most people in the firm will have likely heard about the issues and are eager to give their opinions. Because the area of brand confusion usually surrounds consumers and everyone is a consumer, it is likely that people are eager to give their opinions.

Finally, one should ensure that one's lawyer shows up for court. In an appeal case, *Canadian Schenley Distilleries Ltd. v. Canada's Manitoba Distillery Ltd.* (1975), the respondent's lawyer did not appear. The judge concluded that Canadian Schenley attached no importance or significance to the trademark and that it had lost interest in supporting the validity of the mark. The issue was whether consumers would confuse Tsarevitch with Tovarich for the product category of vodka. The judge discounted the consumer research because the data were collected only in Montreal and not from consumers across the country. He referred to the research as a poll, although it was not. This was clearly an erroneous conclusion, but counsel was not there to defend the research. This case has left a precedent for market research that is incorrect.

SUMMARY

The laws dealing with trademark infringement vary from country to country. The points to be considered in testing for the likelihood of confusion are numerous and may not all apply to any one case. The main overall point to consider is: Does the alleged imitating trademark cause the consumer to think about the original brand and derive inferences from its presence? In other words, is there confusion in the broadest sense of the word?

Designing research to determine consumer confusion is usually a difficult task due to time constraints, confidentiality, and the need for extremely carefully worded questions. Measuring actual confusion by consumer choice behavior is preferred to measuring opinions. In addition to choice behavior, it is also useful to determine specific motivations behind the behavior to get an understanding of what led to the confusion.

An important step in research on brand confusion is to determine the number of people needed for the study. This is an extremely difficult concept to demonstrate and explain in the courtroom as not all involved will understand the techniques of statistical sampling. A novice of statistics will not know that there is an inverse relationship between sample size and critical effect. And to determine that sample size, the critical effect needs to be determined or estimated in advance. The critical effect outlines the proportion of the population that needs to be confused in order to find confusion in the marketplace. In taking averages from previous court cases, an estimate of 20 percent to 25 percent is given by Preston (1990).

Those who are not versed in statistics generally believe that the more people surveyed or sampled, the better the research. This is not the case. The marginal information received after a certain sample size may be without weight. The sample size for a 20 percent confusion level, 95 percent power, at a $p < 0.05$ error rate is approximately 265 people. This all assumes some randomness of the sample and a one-tailed test. In any event, providing information in the context of criterion levels of confusion may provide a better understanding of the confidence given to relatively small sample sizes.

Just as critical as the number of people sampled is the type of people sampled. Despite the fact that courts have ruled that there is no need for samples to be representative of national probability samples, or to include only users of the product, or only those exposed to media running the advertisement (Preston 1990), it is preferable to be as close to these points as possible. Research for consumer reactions is different from research for public opinion polls. Unfortunately, due to the overwhelming abundance of political party research in the form of polling, polling is sometimes considered by those not knowledgeable in marketing research to be the norm or the correct way to gather information. When data are collected in one location, it may be devalued by those who do not understand the generalizability of consumer research gathered using less than random samples of the entire population. Small test markets in localized geographic areas are the norm in market research. Test marketing provides marketing managers with data that are good enough to make decisions with. Random probability samples are not practical, perhaps impossible, and certainly not necessary.

With respect to the other two points on the type of sample, it may be extremely desirable, if not necessary, to have respondents who are users or aware of the product category. It is important that the respondent has the knowledge to respond accurately to the questions of investigation. Many court cases are judged to be flawed based on inappropriate samples.

There are various techniques to evaluate brand imitation. The particular technique chosen should correspond to the specific problem at hand. The research does not necessarily have to take place in a natural purchase environment. Tests of perception often involve laboratory settings that are set up to provide the controls to measure the degree of imitation with reliable precision. Field experiments in the way of prompted or natural shopping provide very conservative tests of confusion with respect to consumer purchase behavior.

Despite the need for some quantification of the level of confusion, courts are often swayed by some very qualitative experiences on the part of consumers. Videotaping focus groups or detailed recorded in-depth interviews of customers often bring life to unexciting statistical information. Everyone can understand and relate to experiences told by others. Other useful anecdotal information presented to the court that provide understandable concrete evidence of confusion are misdirected mail and/or phone calls. Advertising that shows one brand but labels it as another is also an example of confusion through a secondary source.

The general objective in testing for brand imitation is to determine how similar the consumer perceives the two objects in question. Gathering data for the court room must be a careful process. Because judges and lawyers usually are not trained in the nuances of statistics, it is up to the researchers to convey their information in a clear and simple manner. This may be a difficult task. Recently, courts have taken to approving consumer research methodology before it is carried out. The research methodology is submitted to the judge before the data are collected. The judge decides whether the questions, the sample, and the procedure are indeed unbiased. This pre-approval before data collection is the ideal and should lead to a more efficient decision-making process as to the acceptability of the resulting data.

REFERENCES

A & M Pet Products Inc. v. Pieces Inc. and Royal K-9, Southwest United States District Court, Central District of Los Angeles (1989).

Allen, M. J. (1993). The role of actual confusion evidence in trademark infringement litigation. *Trademark Reporter, Vol.83*, 267–304.

American Cyanamid Co. v. United States Rubber Co., United States Court of Customs and Patent Appeals, 53 C.C. P.A. 994, 356 F.2d 1008 (1966).

Amstar Corp. v. Domino's Pizza Inc., 615 F.2d 252, 205 USPQ 969 (CA 5 1980), rehg denied 617 F.2d (CA 5, 1980, Cert denied 449 US 899, 208 USPQ 464 (1980)).

Boal, R. B. (1983). Techniques for ascertaining likelihood of confusion and the meaning of advertising communications. *Trademark Reporter, Vol. 73*, 405–35.

Bonynge, R. (1962). Trademark surveys and techniques and their use in litigation. *Trademark Reporter, Vol. 52*, 363–77.

Canadian Schenley Distilleries Ltd. v. Canada's Manitoba Distillery Ltd., 25 C.P.R. (2d) 1 (F.C.T.D.) (1975).

Chumura Kraemer, H., and Thiemann, S. (1987). *How Many Subjects?: Statistical Power Analysis in Research*. Newbury Park, Calif: Sage Publications.

Coca-Cola Co. v. Tropicana Prods., Inc., 538 F. Supp. 1091, 1096 (S.D.N.Y. 1982), rev'd, 690 F.2d 312, 317 (2d Cir. 1982).

Crespi, I. (1987). Surveys as legal evidence. *Public Opinion Quarterly, Vol. 51*, 84–91.

Day, R. L. (1974). Measuring preferences. In R. E. Ferber (ed.), *Handbook of Marketing Research*. New York: McGraw Hill.

Donovan, R. (1987). *Brand Detectability Research*. Donovan Research, Perth, Australia.

Exxon Corp. v. Texas Motor Exchange of Houston Inc., 628 F2d 500 (5th Cir.) (1980).

Federal Glass Co. v. Corning Glass Works, TMTAB 162 USPQ 279 (1969).

General Motors Corp. v. Cadillac Marine and Boat Co. (WD Mich), 226 F. Supp 716, 140 USPQ 447 (1964).

Glamorene Products Corp. v. Boyle-Midway Inc., 188 USPQ 145 158–59 (SDNY) (1975).

Grotrian, Helfferich, Schultz Steinweg Nach v. Steinway and Sons (1975, CA2 NY) 523 F2d 1331, 186 USPQ 436.

Harlequin Enterprises Ltd. v. Gulf & Western Corp., 644 F2d 946, 949 210 USPQ 1 (CA 2) (1981).

Hartford House Ltd. v. Hallmark Cards Inc., CA (Colo), 846 F2d 1268—Fed Cts. 815, 862; Trade Reg 43, 334, 576, 626 (1986).

Helene Curtis Industries Inc. v. Church & Dwight Co. Inc., 560 F2d 1325, 1331, 195 USPQ 218 (CA 7) (1977).

Hershey Foods Corp. v. Cerreta, TMTAB, 195 USPQ 246 (1977).

Hogan and Another v. Koala Dundee Pty. Ltd and Others, 83 A.L.R. 187 (Federal Court of Australia, Pincus, J.) (1988).

Humble Oil and Refining Co. v. American Oil Co. (1969, CA8 Mo), 405 F 2d 803, 160 USPQ 289, cert den 395 US 905, 23 L Ed 2d 218, 89 S Ct 1745, 161 USPQ 832.

Ideal Toy Corp. v. Kenner Products Div. of General Mills Fun Group Inc., 433 F Supp 291, 308, 197 USPQ 738, 752 (SDNY) (1977).

IMS Ltd. v. International Medical Systems Inc., USPQ 2d 1268, 1274–75 (EDNY) (1986).

International Milling Co. v. Robin Hood Popcorn Co., 110 USPQ 368, 46 TMR 1306, 1308 (1956).

Ives Laboratories Inc. v. Darby Drug Co. Inc., 601 F2d 631, 634, 202 USPQ 548 (CA 2 1979), on remand 488 F Supp 394, 206 USPQ 238 (EDNY 1980), revd 638 F2d 538, 209 USPQ 449 (CA 2 1981), revd 72 TMR 104, 214 USPQ1 (US 1982).

Jacoby, J. (1985). Survey and field experimental evidence. In S. M. Kassin and L. S. Wrightsman (eds.), *The Psychology of Evidence and Trial Procedure*. Beverly Hills, Calif.: Sage Publications, 175–200.

Jenkins Bros. v. Newman Hender & Co. (1961) 48 CCPA 995, 289 F2d 675, 129 U.S.PQ 355.

Jockey International Inc. v. Burkard (1975, SD Cal) 185 USPQ 201.

Kapferer, J. N. and Thoenig, J. C. (1991). Les consommateurs face a la copie. *Prodimarques*. Paris, France: Association pour la Promotion at la Diffusion des Marques.

Kapferer, J. N. (1993). Brand confusion: Empirical study of a legal concept. Working paper, HEC Graduate School of Management, Paris, France.

Leiser, A. W., and Schwartz, C. R. (1983). Techniques for ascertaining whether a term is generic. *Trademark Reporter, Vol. 73*, 376–90.

Levy, S. J., and Rook, D. W. (1981). Brands, trademarks, and the law. In B. M. Enis and K. J. Roering (eds.), *Review of Marketing 1981*. Chicago: American Marketing Association, pp. 185–90.

McWilliam's Wines Pty. Ltd. v. McDonald's System of Australia Pty. Ltd., Fed. Ct. of Australia Gen. Divn. (1980).

Mead Data Central Inc. v. Toyota Motor Sales, U.S.A. Inc., 702 F. Supp 1031 9 USPQ2d 1442 (SDNY) revd 875 F2d 1026, 10 USPQ2d 1961 (CA2 1989) (1988).

Miaoulis, G., and D'Amato, N. (1978). Consumer confusion: Trademark infringement. *Journal of Marketing* (April), 48–55.

Morgan, F. (1990). Judicial standards for survey research: An update and guidelines. *Journal of Marketing, Vol. 54* (January), 59–70.

National Football League v. Governor of the State of Delaware, 435 F Supp 1372, 1379, 195 USPQ 803, 807 (D. Del) (1977).

National Football League Properties Inc. v. Wichita Falls Sportswear Inc., 532 F Supp 651, 215 USPQ 175 (W.D. Wash) (1982).

Oppenheim, S. C., Weston, G. E., Maggs, P. B., and Schechter, R. E. (1983). *Unfair Trade Practices and Consumer Protection: Cases and Comments*. St. Paul, Minn.: West Publishing Co.

Parkdale Custom Built Furniture Proprietary Limited v. Puxu Proprietary Limited, High Court of Australia (1981–1982).

Pattishall, B. W. (1959). Reaction test evidence in trade identity cases. *Trademark Reporter, Vol. 49*, 145–74.

Preston, I. L. (1989a). The Federal Trade Commission's identification of implications as constituting deceptive advertising. *Cincinnati Law Review, Vol. 57*, 1243–1309.

———. (1989b). False or deceptive advertising under the Lanham Act: Analysis of factual findings and types of evidence. *Trademark Reporter, Vol. 79*, 508–53.

———. (1990). The definition of deceptiveness in advertising and other commercial speech. *Catholic University Law Review, Vol. 39*, No. 4 (Summer), 1035–79.

Price Pfister Inc. v. Mundo Corp. et al., Superior Court of the State of California (1989).

Purofied Down Products Corp. v. Puro Down International of New Jersey Corp.,
        530 F Supp 134, 135 fn 2, 218 USPQ 720, 721 (EDNY) (1982).

Reiner, J. P. (1983). The universe and the sample: How good is good
        enough? *Trademark Reporter, Vol. 73*, 366–75.

RJR Foods Inc. v. White Rock Corp. (1978, SD NY) 201 USPQ 578, Affd (CA2
        NY) 603 F2d 1058, 203 USPQ 401.

Robin, A., and Barnaby, H. B. (1973). Trademark surveys—heads you
        lose, tails they win. *Trade Mark Forum, Vol. 73*, 436–45.

Sears, Roebuck and Co. v. Allstate Driving School Inc., 376 U.S. 225, 84 S. Ct.
        784, 11 L.Ed.2d 661 (1964).

Sears, Roebuck and Co. v. Allstate Driving School Inc. (1969, ED NY) 301 F
        Supp 4, 163 USPQ 335.

Smith v. Sturm, Ruger & Co. Inc., 39 Wash. App. 740, 695 F2d 600 (1985).

Smith, J. G., Snyder, W. S., Swire, J. B., Donegan, T. J., Jr., and Ross, I.
        (1983). Legal standards for consumer survey research. *Journal of
        Advertising Research, Vol. 23*, No. 5 (October/November), 19–35.

Sorensen, R. C. (1983). Survey research execution in trademark litigation:
        Does practise make perfection? *Trademark Reporter, Vol. 73*, 349–
        65.

Squirt Co. v. Seven-Up Co., 207 USPQ 12 (ED Mo), aff'd 628 F2d 1086, 207
        USPQ 897 (CA 8 1980) (1979).

Valerio, P. (1992). Case histories in the use of t-scopes in design research.
        Unpublished manuscript, Landor and Associates, San Fran-
        cisco.

Weight Watchers International v. The Stouffer Corp., No. 88 Civ 7062 (MBM),
        United States D (1990).

Wells Fargo & Co. v. Wells Fargo Construction Co., 619 F Supp 710, 712–3 229
        USPQ 938 (D. Ariz) (1985).

Wickens, T. D. (1991). Elementary signal detection theory. Unpublished
        manuscript, UCLA, Los Angeles.

Zippo Mfg. Co. v. Rogers Imports, Inc. (1963, SDNY) 216 F. Supp. 670, 137
        USPQ 413.

Summary and Unanswered Questions

Brand imitation is a world-wide problem. Protecting one's brand identity may not be an easy task. Preventing and stopping brand imitators may be even more bothersome, as evidenced in a 1990 survey among European companies manufacturing branded goods. The results of the survey showed that more than 80 percent of the respondents had seen some of their products imitated at least once within the preceding five years, yet only half of them had taken legal steps against the imitators. Manufacturers cited cumbersome procedures, high costs, and uncertainty of outcomes as the main reasons for not defending their rights (FAIR PLAY 1994: 15). The questions to be asked are: What is lost by allowing brand imitators to the market? What is to be gained by preventing or stopping brand imitation?

The decision to proceed with legal action might depend on the size of the original brand's firm and the size of the imitator brand's firm. When the original firm is a large corporation, it might be more likely to take legal action against any imitating firms immediately. These large corporations are likely to have in-house legal counsel. When the original is a small firm, it may be less likely to take legal action in the beginning. A small firm might be more likely to seek cooperation by the offending imitator company out of the court-room. If no solution is found out of court, the small firm might then proceed with legal action.

When the imitator is a direct competitor, as well as a retail distributor of the original brand, the legal journey is less clear. It may be that manufacturers are reluctant to go after retail store imitator brands because of fear of losing shelf space in the retailer's store, or even worse, being dropped from the retail chain's distribution system (Kapferer 1992). To date, no empirical evidence exists to support this speculation.

If manufacturers are afraid of retailer imitators, ignoring them may not be the best strategy. Monetary evidence to date favors the prosecution of imitators. Lost sales and dilution of brand image cannot be beneficial to the original brand. Clearly, more research is needed to document the costs and benefits to the original brand under conditions of legal action as opposed to no legal action.

WINNERS AND LOSERS

An attempt was made to measure the value of trademarks through stock market data of corporations involved in trademark litigation (Bhagat and Umesh 1992). The premise of the study was that lawsuits are filed to protect trademarks and that is a positive signal to the market that the firm is serious about fighting brand imitation in the marketplace. The lawsuit is seen as a firm's signal blaming another company for any erosion of its sales or market share.

Bhagat and Umesh postulated that a corporation would decide to file a lawsuit to protect its trademark or brand name if the expected value of the settlement exceeded the expected legal and non-legal costs. The benefits to the corporation might be: 1) monetary damages paid by the defendant; 2) court-ordered injunctive relief; 3) a settlement that might require the defendant to stop infringing on the plaintiff's trademark or brand name; and 4) possible prevention of future imitators. These benefits might be reflected in the price of the corporation's stock price. In contrast, the imitator is seen as having little long-term benefits and many costs in defending the lawsuit.

Therefore, the researchers hypothesized that the plaintiff shareholder wealth should increase and the defendant shareholder wealth should decrease with the filing of a trademark lawsuit. Using data available between 1975 and 1990, the study concluded that trademarks have value. The mere filing of a lawsuit led to a drop in the stock value of the defendant firm. When the verdict went against the defendant the loss was considerable, but a favorable verdict did not lead to a gain in returns. The researchers deduced that lawsuits produce a net negative effect for the defendant. However, the stock losses by the defendant were not matched by stock gains for the plaintiff.

This study was restricted to firms with public holdings and did not address the more common occurrence of brand imitations by small private companies. The costs of fighting a lawsuit may be heavily weighted by legal costs. Fletcher (1991) reports legal fees of up to $95,803.60 for a bench trial of four days involving two similar names. Small firms may not be able to absorb legal fees, and any legal action may lead to bankruptcy for them. Therefore, small firms may be highly motivated to settle out of court and immediately stop the imitation process. However, when a small firm is the original and a larger firm is the infringer, the legal action is a much riskier process due to the legal costs involved.

RELIEF IN INFRINGEMENT CASES

Relief can be in the form of injunctive relief against future infringement or damages (including lost profits) from past infringement. Recovery of damages seems to have been difficult in the past, but recent cases in the United States are showing a different trend (see Exhibit 7.1).

The courts may choose a common-sense approach to awarding damages. In the Big O tire case, Goodyear was required to pay Big O 25 percent of its advertising budget spent promoting the major tire company's Big Foot Line. This amount was near $5 million. In a Utah case, Godfathers Pizza opened several company-owned outlets under the Godfathers name in full knowledge of the existence of a Godfathers Restaurant in Salt Lake City. The restaurant sued for name infringement. The judge ruled that Godfathers Pizza could continue to use the name if it paid Godfathers Restaurant 25

Exhibit 7.1
Recent Awards in Trademark Infringement Cases

Case	Amount	Comment
Arachnid Inc. v. Medalist Marketing (1991)	$100,000	Awarded by jury — based on imitators' profits
Broan Mfg. Co. Inc. v. Associated Distributions Inc. (1991)	$523,000	Awarded by jury — imitator judged lower quality and possible harm to purchaser
Break-Away Tours Inc. v. British Caledonian Airways (1988)	$1	Injunction; recovery compensatory — not penal
Celebrity Service International Inc. v. Celebrity World Inc. (1988)	$248,745	Based on 3 times lost revenue from subscriptions
Fax Express Inc. v. Halt (1988)	$687,500	Based on 3 times lost revenue, plus $200,000 loss of goodwill and reputation
Halem Industries Inc. v. Fasco Industries Inc. (1988)	$44,000	Awarded by jury
Limelight Prods. Inc. v. Limelite Studios Inc. (1992)	$2,500,000	Jury awarded for damages
Sands, Taylor and Wood v. Quaker Oats Co. (1990)	$24,730,000	Court inferred that 10% of the brand's success resulted from infringement period. 10% of profits equals damages.
Sturm, Ruger & Co. Inc. v. Arcadia Machine Tool Inc. (1988)	$2,804,924	Based on lost profits
Walt Disney Co. v. Powell (1988)	$15,000	Based on defendants' sales, no records kept
Zazu Designs v. L'Oreal S.A. (1988)	$1,000,000	Based on lost profits, advertising costs and punitive damages

percent of its total advertising expenditures in the Utah market each year. This amounted to $50,000. That 25 percent could be used by the restaurant for advertising to clarify in people's minds the difference between the two companies or the restaurant could pocket the 25 percent. The restaurant was now assured of a profit (Hunt 1990).

In 1988 Bette Midler successfully sued the Ford Motor Company and its advertising agency, Young and Rubican, for $400,000 for the commercial exploitation of her voice without her consent. Hot on the heels of that case, a Los Angeles court awarded damages of $2.475 million to the singer Tom Waits after deciding that the use of a Waits sound-alike in a corn chips radio commercial was an "improper misappropriation of identity" (Using the Law 1991).

In *Tavern Pizza Restaurant v. S. & L. Food Services Inc.*, the dispute was over recipes for pizza. A jury was used to decide the case, rather than a judge. The jurors never tasted either pizza, but after comparing written recipes they unanimously sided with Tavern Pizza restaurant and awarded $465,000 in damages (Woo 1992).

In another food case, a jury awarded $100,000 in damages to Chocolates a la Carte after finding Presidential Confection guilty of copying the sea-shell shapes of its competitor (Felsenthal 1992). There may be an advantage in trial by jury rather than judge in that juries seem to award damages to the original creator more often.

The U.S. Supreme Court ended a five-year battle between Taco Cabana and Two Pesos restaurant chains. It upheld an appeals court decision that required Two Pesos to alter the appearance of its restaurants radically and pay $3.7 million to Taco Cabana ("Supreme Court affirms" 1992). This was an interesting case in that the court held that the plaintiffs had to prove only that their business' appearance was "inherently distinctive," not that customers viewed the physical characteristics as unique and defining elements of its identity. The court further stated that the inherently distinctive elements do not have to be registered to be protected. The interpretation of this statement by industry seems to be that owners of an original trade dress will no longer have to bring extensive consumer studies into court to show that patrons could be confused about the ownership of similar packaged brands. Consumers do not have to be deceived; they just have to perceive similarity and derive similar expectations.

The distinctive elements for Taco Cabana were its "festive eating atmosphere," including "patio areas decorated with artifacts, bright colors, paintings and murals" as well as colored exterior "neon stripes," striped awnings and umbrellas, a particular counter shape, roof line, and menu configuration. The judgment required Two Pesos to switch to white neon, solid-colored awnings, and grey or white interiors, as well as to alter its roof lines and post signs for one year admitting that it had copied Taco Cabana.

The seriousness of the courts in addressing trademark infringement is also evident in *Merriam-Webster v. Random House* ("Merriam-Webster wins" 1991). Both companies' dictionaries had red covers with the name "Webster's" in similar white typeface on the cover and spine. Merriam-Webster has been using the same cover since 1973. Random House, which originally called its dictionary The Random House Dictionary, changed its name and began using a red cover in 1991. The jury awarded Merriam-Webster $1.7 million in compensatory damages and $500,000 in punitive damages. The judge then ordered the compensatory award to be more than doubled to $3.5 million and personally redesigned the infringing book jacket himself, specifying requirements for typesize, color, and word arrangement for a new Random House jacket.

Sometimes the relief in the form of damages is merely symbolic. In *Walt Disney Co. v. Triple Five Corp.*, Disney wanted to stop the firm from using the name "Fantasyland" for its amusement area and hotel in West Edmonton Mall, Canada, and sought one dollar in damages (Coulter 1992). After the Canadian courts ordered the mall to stop using the name Fantasyland, the case was unsuccessfully appealed.

Summary

It generally appears that brand imitation is an expensive risk to the imitating company. While initial profits from such a strategy make it appear to be worthwhile, the resulting legal fees and judgments could determine the closure of the imitating company. Prior court findings suggest that original brands have little to lose in protecting their brand identity against imitators in the marketplace. The data also suggest that imitation can be an expensive and risky strategy by competitors. One conclusion might be that original brands should always protect their identity and that imitation is only a short-term strategy that may prove very costly to the firm. The clear winner, in any case, is the legal firm hired to represent those involved.

OTHER DEFENSIVE STRATEGIES

One strategy that is open to packaged goods, when the look or Gestalt of the package is imitated, is to change the look or Gestalt of the package. Many firms would rather switch than fight. When a highly successful brand finds that other brands (especially store brands) have copied the color and design of its product, it may design a new look to distance itself from its imitators and avoid legal action. Brands such as Oil of Olay beauty products have changed their package. They advertise the new "updated" look and consumers soon learn about the new package through the advertising they are exposed to.

There are brands which may not change the package, but change the color or look of their product. For example, Fiberglass Pink Insulation could change its product to variegated pink rather than solid pink. It could then advertise the "Pink Zebra" rather than the Pink Panther. Constantly updating and changing one's look may keep the brand imitators at bay. If an imitator does choose to follow the original's change, the court case against it for brand imitation would be even stronger.

KEEPING BRAND IMITATION IN PERSPECTIVE

It is so easy to be different in the marketplace that it may actually be unethical to be similar. Companies that are innovative and invest in their image should be able to keep their image to themselves. They do not have to share it. The purpose in writing this book is to make people aware of the various issues, not to serve as a guide on creating imitators. Yet there is danger of creating more imitation, not less, by providing information. As my colleague Dennis Rook commented,

There is obviously an audience for the book among those interested in protecting their intellectual property innovation. There is also, probably, an audience among manufacturers who pursue imitative strategies. *Both* are interested in the question: How far can you go before legal infringement occurs? This duality is the source of considerable controversy, yet it seems central to the (sometimes competing) issues of property protection, fair competition, and consumer protection.

These are extremely important thoughts that have not totally escaped me while writing this book. I have had several conversations with brand managers about dealing with imitators. When the imitator is another relatively large company with a product not too significantly different in quality, that imitator evolves into a competitor. The evolution takes place with the imitator changing some of the offending strategy and developing its own advertising and positioning. Some of the new approaches by the imitator may even be copied by the original. Hence, in some rare cases, the original and imitator learn from each other.

Some companies view brand imitation strictly as a legal problem in the beginning. It is not until the imitator continues on the market for some time that the brand imitator becomes a marketing problem for the original. That may be because the originating firm believes that if the imitator is inferior, it will disappear because the consumer will not buy it. That is, the consumer will determine the importance of the imitator to the market by sales and market share. If the brand is inferior, consumers will not buy it and the imitator will have a short shelf life. However, if the imitator brand comes close to matching the quality of the original and gains significant market share, there is a problem with imitation. Attention is then paid to the original brand's declining market share and sales.

There are several problems with this strategy from the consumer's perspective. If the product is inferior, the consumer loses and the image of the product category as a whole may be diminished. It is vital to prosecute the infringers with poor quality products. Poor quality helps no one. If the product is of equal quality and is sold cheaper, the consumer may benefit in the economic sense. The company may also lose in the economics of lost sales.

The dilemma in direct brand imitation, when product quality is taken into account, is that what is good for the customer is not necessarily good for the corporation. Do we have one set of judicial standards for good imitators and another set of standards for poor imitators? Or are all imitators treated equally, irrespective of the quality offered to the consumer? These are questions yet to be answered with respect to brand imitation.

REFERENCES

Arachnid Inc. v. Medalist Marketing Corp., 18 USPQ 2d 1941 (WD Wash) (1991).

Bette Midler v. Ford Motor Co., 849 F2d 460 (9th Cir.) (1988).

Bhagat, S., and Umesh, U. N. (1992). The market value of trademarks measured via trademark litigation. Marketing Science Institute, Cambridge, Mass., 92–131.

Big O Tire Dealers v. Goodyear Tire and Rubber, US Ct of Appeals, Tenth Circuit, 561 F.2d 1365 (1977).

Break-Away Tours Inc. v. British Caledonian Airways, 704 F Supp 178, 8 USPQ 2d 1140 (SD Calif) (1988).

Broan Mfg. Co. Inc. v. Associated Distributors Inc., 923 F2d 1232, 17 USPQ 2d 1617 (CA 6) (1991).

Celebrity Service International Inc. v. Celebrity World Inc., 9 USPQ 2d 1673 (SDNY) (1988).

Coulter, D. (1992, August 12). WEM wins reprieve in fantasyland battle. *Edmonton Journal*, B1.

FAIR PLAY (1994), Lego Group, Billund, Denmark: Lego Group.

Fax Express Inc. v. Halt, 708 F. Supp 649, 8 USPQ 2d 1618 (ED Pa) (1988).

Felsenthal, E. (1992, July 16). Ice sculptors view this outcome as a means to a lasting legacy. *Wall Street Journal*, B1.

Fletcher, A. L. (1991). Trademark infringement and unfair competition in courts of general jurisdiction. *Trademark Reporter, Vol. 81*, 718–91.

Halem Industries Inc. v. Fasco Industries Inc., 865 F2d 268, 10 USPQ 1319 (CAFC 1988).

Hunt, H. K. (1990). Second-order effects of the FTC initiatives. In P. E. Murphy and W. L. Wilkie (eds.), *Marketing and Advertising*. South Bend, Ind.: University of Notre Dame, pp. 88–93.

Kapferer, J. N. (1992). *Strategic Brand Management*. Londons Kogan Page.

Limelight Prods. Inc. v. Limelite Studios Inc., U.S. District Ct., S.D. Fla., No. 89–965– CIV-Aronvitz (1992).

Merriam-Webster wins doubled award in Random House suit. (1991, November 22). *Publishers Weekly*, p. 13.

Sands, Taylor & Wood v. Quaker Oats Co., 18 USPQ 2d 1457 (ND ILL 1990).

Sturm, Ruger & Co. Inc. v. Arcadia Machine & Tool Inc., 10 USPQ 2d 1522 (CD Calif 1988).

Supreme Court affirms "thou shalt not steal" rule in copycat case. (1992, August 24). *Nation's Restaurant News*.

Taco Bell Pty. Ltd. v. Taco Co. of Australia Inc., Fed. Ct. of Australia, Sydney (1981).

Using the law to smash the competition. (1991). *Marketing*, Australia, 31–33.

Walt Disney Co. v. Powell, 698 F Supp 10, 9 USPQ 2d 1234 (DC 1988).

Woo, J. (1992, September 30). He proved he knew his onions and pepperoni, and sausage, etc. *Wall Street Journal*, B1.

Zazu Designs v. L'Oreal S. A., 9 USPQ 2d 1972 (ND ILL 1988).

Appendix: Brand Imitation and the Law

The protection of brand identity is regulated under the Lanham Act in the United States, under the Trademarks Act in Canada, under the Regulation for Community Trade Mark in Europe, and under the Consumer Protection Act in Australia. The laws are similar, but vary from country to country. Laws and decisions about trademark rights are subject to change over time, and the interpretation of the laws varies within country and from case to case. Specific laws of any country are often retested.

Some general background with respect to the definitions used in the language of the law, the various considerations and interpretations, as well as the spirit of the law are outlined in this Appendix. Because the specifics of each country's laws are subject to change and interpretation over time, laws should be interpreted and dealt with by lawyers, not lay people. The following excerpts from the laws of various countries are intended to provide the reader with some reference points, not legal advice. They are not complete and are heavily edited for ease of reading. The reader is cautioned against using this Appendix in any formal manner. Any errors or omissions are not intended and are the fault of the author.

TRADEMARKS AND THE UNITED STATES

Trademark laws in the United States are outlined under what is commonly known as the Lanham Act or the Trademarks Act of 1946. A recent section was added to deal with false designations of origin or false descriptions of goods (Armstrong 1992). These false claims may be referred to in other countries as passing-off.

Definition of Trademark

A trademark is any mark, word, letter, number, design, picture, or combination thereof in any form of arrangement that:

(a) is adopted and used by a person to denominate goods which he or she markets and is affixed to the goods and;

(b) is not a common or generic name for the goods or a picture of them, or a geographical, personal, or corporate or other association name, or a designation descriptive of the goods or of their quality, ingredients, properties and functions (Trademark Act s.2, 715).

A trade name is any designation that:

(a) is adopted and used by a person to denominate goods which he or she markets or services which he or she renders or a business which he or she conducts, or has to be so used by others; and

(b) through its association with such goods, services, or business, has acquired a special significance as the name thereof (Trademark Act s.2, 716).

Infringement. One infringes another's trademark or trade name if:

(a) without a privilege to do so, he or she uses in his or her business, in the manner of a trademark or trade name, a designation which is identical with or confusingly similar to the other's trademark, though he or she does not use the designation for the purpose of deception; and

(b) the other's interest in his trade name is protected with reference to:
  i)   the goods, services or business in connection with which the actor uses his or her designation, and
  ii)   the markets in which the actor uses the designation;

(c)   the other's trademark is not a clear likeness of a third person's prior and subsisting trademark or trade name in substantially the same market for the same or clearly related goods (Trademark Act s.2, 717).

Passing-Off. The false designations of origin and false descriptions are forbidden as follows.

(a)   Any person who, on or in connection with any goods or services, or any container for goods, uses in commerce any word, term, name, symbol, or device, or any combination thereof, or any false designation of origin, false or misleading description of fact, or false or misleading representation of fact, which:

    i)   is likely to cause confusion, or to cause mistake, or to deceive as to the affiliation, connection, or association of such person with another person, or as to the origin, sponsorship, or approval of his or her goods, services, or commercial activities by another person; or

    ii)   in commercial advertising or promotion, misrepresents the nature, characteristics, qualities, or geographic origin of his or her or another person's goods, services, or commercial activities,

shall be liable in a civil action by any person who believes that he or she is or is likely to be damaged by such act.

Testing for Likelihood of Confusion

The determination of trademark infringement sometimes depends on establishing whether the public has been confused by the alleged infringer. The courts consider various points in testing for likelihood of confusion.

They are:

(a)   the similarity or dissimilarity of the trademarks in their entireties as appearance, sound, connotation, and commercial impression;
(b)   the similarity or dissimilarity and nature of the goods or services as described in an application;
(c)   the similarity or dissimilarity of established, likely-to-continue trade channels;
(d)   the conditions under which and buyers to whom sales are made, i.e., impulse versus careful, sophisticated shopping;
(e)   the fame of the prior mark (sales, advertising, length of use);
(f)   the number and nature of similar marks in use on similar goods;
(g)   the nature and extent of any actual confusion;

(h)   the length of time during and conditions under which there has been concurrent use without evidence of actual confusion;

(i)   the variety of goods on which a mark is or is not used (house mark, family mark, product mark);

(j)   the market must interface between applicant and the owner of a prior mark:

    i)   a mere consent to register to use,

    ii)   agreement provisions designed to preclude confusion, i.e., limitations on continued use of the marks by each party,

    iii)   assignment of mark, application, registration, and goodwill of the related business,

    iv)   laches and estoppel attributable to owner of prior mark and indicative of lack of confusion;

(k)   the extent to which applicant has a right to exclude others from use of its mark on their goods;

(l)   the extent of potential confusion;

(m)   any other established fact prohibitive of the effect of use (Trademark Act, s.2(d) 159).

Among the different legal jurisdictions in the United States, there is very little agreement on what factors to consider in testing for likelihood of confusion (Fletcher 1989). Some circuits apply equal weight to many factors, some apply equal weight to only a few factors, and some focus on only one or two factors. Each circuit may also consider different factors as the most important.

TRADEMARKS IN CANADA

Any term, symbol, design or combination of these that identifies a business or a product is called a trademark in Canada and is protected under the Federal Trademarks Act (1985). A trademark must be registered to be protected under the statute. Exclusive rights and protection are granted for use throughout Canada and in other countries party to the International Trademark Agreement. This protection is granted for fifteen years and is renewable (Yates 1989).

Definition of a Trademark

In Chapter T-13, section 2 of the Trademarks Act, a trademark is defined as a mark that is used for the purpose of distinguishing goods or services that are of a defined standard with respect to:

(a) the character or quality of the goods or services;

(b) the working conditions under which the goods have been produced or the services performed;

(c) the class of persons by whom the goods have been produced or the services performed; or

(d) the area within which the goods have been produced or the services performed

from goods or services that are not of that defined standard.

Confusion

When the distinguishing aspect is not met, it is said that the goods or services are confused. The word "confusing," when applied as an adjective to a trademark or trade name, means that the use of a trademark or trade name causes confusion with another trademark or trade name in the same area. This confusion would be likely to lead to the inference that the goods and services associated with:

(a) those trademarks;

(b) the trademark and those associated with the business carried on under the trade name;

(c) the business carried on under the trade name and those associated with the trademark

are manufactured, sold, leased, hired, or performed by the same person, whether or not the wares or services are of the same general class (Trademarks Act Chap. T-13, s. 6).

Consideration of What Is Confusing. In determining whether trademarks or tradenames are confusing, the court regards the following:

(a) the inherent distinctiveness of the trademarks or trade names and the extent to which they have become known;

(b) the length of time the trademarks or trade names have been in use;

(c) the nature of the wares, services, or business;

(d) the nature of the trade; and

(e)   the degree of resemblance between the trademarks or trade names in appearance or sound or in the ideas suggested by them (Trademarks Act Chap. T-13, s. 6(5)).

Unfair Competition and Prohibited Marks. No person shall:

(a)   make false or misleading statements tending to discredit the business, wares, or services of a competitor;
(b)   direct public attention to his or her wares, services or business in such a way as to cause or likely to cause confusion in Canada, at the time he or she commenced so to direct attention to them, between his or her wares, services, or business and the wares, services or business of another;
(c)   pass off other wares or services as and for those ordered or requested;
(d)   make use, in association with wares or services, of any description that is false in material respect and likely to mislead the public as to:
    i)   the character, quality, quantity, or composition,
    ii)   the geographical origin, or
    iii)   the mode of the manufacture, production or performance
of the wares or services (Chap. T-13, s. 7).

Infringement. The right of the owner of a registered trademark to its exclusive use shall be deemed to be infringed by a person not entitled to its use under this Act who sells, distributes, or advertises wares or services in association with a confusing trademark or trade name, but no registration of a trademark prevents a person from making:

(a)   any bona fide use of his personal name as a trade name; or
(b)   any bona fide use, other than as a trademark,
    i)   of the geographical name of the place of business, or
    ii)   of any accurate description of the character or quality of his wares or services,

in such a manner as is not likely to have the effect of depreciating the value of the goodwill attaching to the trademark (Trademarks Act Chap. T-13, s. 20).

Concurrent Use of Confusing Marks. Where, in any proceedings respecting a registered trademark the registration of which is entitled to protection, it is made to appear to the Federal Court that one of the parties to the proceedings, other than the registered owner of the trademark, had in good faith used a confusing trademark or tradename in Canada before the date of filing of the application for that registration, and the court considers that is not contrary to public interest that the continued use of the confusing trademark or trade name should be permitted in a defined territorial area concurrently with the use of the registered trademark. The Court may order that the other party may continue to use the confusing trademark or trade name within that area with an adequate specified distinction from the registered trademark (Trademarks Act Chap. T-13, s. 21(1)).

Depreciation of Goodwill

No person shall use a trademark registered by another person in a manner that is likely to have the effect of depreciating the value of the goodwill attaching thereto. In any action to the above, the court may decline to order the recovery of damages or profits and may permit the defendant to continue to sell wares marked with the trademark that were in his or her possession or under his or her control at the time the notice was given to him or her that the owner of the registered trademark complained of the use of the trademark (Trademarks Act Chap. T-13, s. 22).

TRADEMARKS AND THE EUROPEAN UNION

At the time of writing this book, the EU had not as yet formalized the collective agreement on trademarks. The Council of European Communities had written a directive relating to trademarks (1989) and an updated version on the working paper (1991). Parts of the working agreement are reproduced for this Appendix.

Definition of a Community Trademark

A community trademark may consist of any signs capable of being represented graphically, particularly words, including personal names, designs, letters, numerals, the shape of goods or of their packaging, provided that such signs are capable of distinguishing the goods or services of one undertaking from those of other undertakings (Trademarks, Dir. 89/104, A. 2).

The Council and the Commission consider that the definition of a trademark does not rule out the possibility:

- of registering as a Community trademark a combination of colours or a single colour;
- of registering in the future, as Community trademarks, sounds, i.e., distinctive audibles,

provided that they are capable of distinguishing the goods or services of one undertaking from those of other undertakings.

The Council and the Commission consider that the word "shape" is also intended to cover the three-dimensional form of goods and that where goods are packaged, the expression "shape of goods" includes the shape of the packaging.

Adoption of this law will make it easier for a trademark to qualify for registration allowing companies to register three-dimensional shapes such as Johnny Walker whiskey bottles which form part of the brand. So a distinctively shaped bottle will become just as registrable as a brand name (Rice 1993).

Ineligible Trademarks. The following shall be refused registration as a trademark:

(a) signs which do not conform to the requirements outlined in defining EU trademarks;
(b) trademarks which are devoid of any distinctive character;
(c) trademarks which consist exclusively of signs or indications which may serve, in trade, to designate the kind, quality, quantity, intended purpose, value, geographical origin, or the time of production of the goods or rendering of the service, or other characteristics of the goods or service;
(d) trademarks which consist exclusively of signs or indications which have become customary to designate the goods or service in the current language or bona fide and established practices of the trade;
(e) signs which consist exclusively of:
   i)   the shape which results from the nature of the goods themselves, or
   ii) the shape of goods which is necessary to obtain a technical result, or
   iii) the shape which gives substantial value to the goods;

(f)   trademarks which are contrary to public policy or to accepted principles of morality;

(g)   trademarks which are of such a nature as to deceive the public, for instance as to the nature, quality, or geographical origin of the goods or service;

(h)   trademarks which have not been authorized by the competent authorities;

(i)   trademarks which include badges, emblems, or escutcheons (Trademarks, Dir. 89/104, A. 3).

Unfair Competition. The Council and the Commission consider that the reference to the law of Member States relating in particular to civil liability and unfair competition is to be construed as including passing-off. Passing-off is a term used in common-law countries such as the United Kingdom. It occurs when one person presents goods or services in a way which is likely to injure the business or goodwill of another person, for example by causing the public to believe that they are goods or services associated with that other person. In order to succeed in an action for passing-off, a plaintiff must show that the way his or her goods or services are presented by the defendant is likely to be injured by that confusion. It is not however necessary to show that the defendant intended to mislead or confuse the public.

Licensing. There are five points put forth by the commission with respect to licensing:

1. A community trademark may be licensed for some or all of the goods or services for which it is registered and for the whole or part of the community. A license may be exclusive or non-exclusive.

2. The proprietor of a Community trademark may invoke the rights conferred by that trademark against a licensee who contravenes any provision in the licensing contract with regard to duration, the form covered by the registration in which the trademark may be used, the scope of the goods or services for which the license is granted, the territory in which the trademark may be affixed, or the quality of the goods manufactured or of the services provided by the licensee.

3. Without prejudice to the provisions of the licensing contract, the licensee may bring proceedings for infringement of a Community trademark only if its proprietor consents thereto. However, the holder of an exclusive license may bring such proceedings if the proprietor of the

trademark, after having been given notice to do so, does not bring infringement proceedings.

4. A licensee shall, for the purpose of obtaining compensation for damage suffered, be entitled to intervene in an infringement action brought by the proprietor of the Community trademark.

5. On request of one of the parties the grant or transfer of a license in respect of a Community trademark shall be entered in the Register and published (EC Regulation, 4595/91, A. 22(21)).

AUSTRALIAN TRADEMARK LAW

Reference to trademark infringement may be found under Section 53 of the Consumer Protection Act of Australia with respect to false or misleading representations. The law states that a corporation shall not, in trade or commerce, in connection with the supply or possible supply of goods or services, or in connection with the promotion by any means of the supply or use of goods or services:

(a) falsely represent that the goods or services are of a particular standard, quality, value, grade, composition, style, or model, or have had a particular history or particular previous use;

(b) represent that goods or services have sponsorship, approval, performance characteristics, accessories, uses or benefits they do not have;

(c) represent that the corporation has a sponsorship, approval or affiliation it does not have;

(d) make a false or misleading representation concerning the place of origin of goods.

REFERENCES

Armstrong, Joel S. (1992). Secondary meaning "in the making" in trademark infringement actions under section 43(9) of the Lanham Act. *George Mason University Law Review*, 14 (Summer), No. 3, 603–35.

Consumer Protection Act (1977). Sec. 52A(3), Australia.

EC regulation on the community trademark (1991, March 4). Draft paper. Council of European Communities.

Fletcher, Anthony L. (1989). Trademark infringement and unfair compe-
        tition in courts of general jurisdiction. *Trademark Reporter, Vol.
        79,* 794–882.

Lanham Act (1988), 15 U:S:C: 1051–1127.

Rice, Robert (1993, November 19). Boost for London's EC trademarks
        role. *Financial Times,* p. 12.

Trademarks Act. R.S.C. (1985) Chap. T-13, s. 1., Canada.

Trademarks in the EEC: Directive 89/104 (1989). *Common Market Reporter,*
        4725–1 to 11.

Yates, Richard A. (1989). *Business Law in Canada.* Scarborough, Ontario:
        Prentice-Hall Canada.

Index of Cases

Index

About the Author

JUDITH LYNNE ZAICHKOWSKY is an associate professor of marketing at the Faculty of Business Administration, Simon Fraser University, in Canada who is best known for her work on involvement, a motivational construct within the field of marketing. Dr. Zaichkowsky has been actively researching consumers since the early 1970s and has published works on many facets of consumer behavior.